A SEASON IN STRATHGLASS

A SEASON

IN

STRATHGLASS

John Fowler

BIRLINN

First published in 2013 by
Birlinn Limited
West Newington House
10 Newington Road
Edinburgh
EH9 1QS

www.birlinn.co.uk

Photographs by Catherine Fowler and the author

ISBN: 978 1 78027 157 6

British Library Cataloguing-in-Publication Data
A catalogue record for this book is available from the British Library.

Typeset by Edderston Book Design, Peebles
Printed and bound by Grafica Veneta
www.graficaveneta.com

for Alasdair and Sheila

INTRODUCTION

Fifteen years or so ago, I walked across the Highlands with Catherine, now my wife. We went from the Beauly Firth in the east to the west coast and stopped for the night at a remote hostel beyond Loch Affric. I made supper but, before the spaghetti was on the table, Catherine, new to walking, had fallen fast asleep, her head on the table.

Pinned to the noticeboard in the kitchen was a brief history of the area, including this:

> Affric was one of a group of glens which were traditional routes from west to east.
>
> Twelve shepherds and two gamekeepers and their families lived in West Affric in the 1850s. When cheap imports of refrigerated mutton made shepherding uneconomic and high rents could be charged from sporting tenants, West Affric became part of the massive deer forest of a Canadian railway magnate called Winans . . .

No one lives in West Affric nowadays except for hostel wardens who come and go. As for Winans the railway magnate (not Canadian but American), there will be more to tell.

My old guidebook to the mountains of the western Highlands declares that 'Strathfarrar, Cannich and Affric are three of the longest glens in Scotland and are universally regarded as her three most beautiful'. There have been dramatic changes since the words were written but even now, in spite of widespread flooding for hydroelectricity and blanket conifer afforestation, they still ring true today.

Down these three glens pour three rivers which merge at length as the

River Glass, whose dark waters flow for several miles through a flat valley or strath, hence the name Strathglass. For a while, over a decade, I made many visits to the three glens and the strath of Glass, always lured back by the grandeur of the scenery and the character of the people who live there. As a kind of shorthand, I came to style the whole area in my mind simply as 'Affric', a name that has a particular resonance for me. It was the first of the glens I got to know, a place of craggy hills, ancient pinewoods and many waters, almost too theatrical to be true. And so, when I used to say, on leaving home, 'I'm going to Affric,' my wife and friends knew what I meant and where I'd be. Sometimes Catherine came with me.

Mostly I came by way of Beauly. Beauly, *beau lieu* – 'bonny place' – and so it is. It's a small country town set in a pastoral landscape half an hour's drive from Inverness. It has a modest sense of style and a pleasant air of gentility. Here the River Glass, which started life as the Affric deep in the hills of the west, briefly becomes the River Beauly in the last stage of its long life. The hills are left behind and the sea is close. Another approach is from Drumnadrochit, a ragged village on Loch Ness where tourists decant in hope of sighting the monster. The shop tills there ring an anthem to Nessie.

This narrative is based on diaries I kept during my time in Affric and Strathglass. Because the period covers several years, the result is kaleidoscopic or impressionistic and I've not attempted to keep to a strict chronology. But I think it holds together.

It's some time since my last spell in Affric and there have been changes since. You'll find some in the postscript.

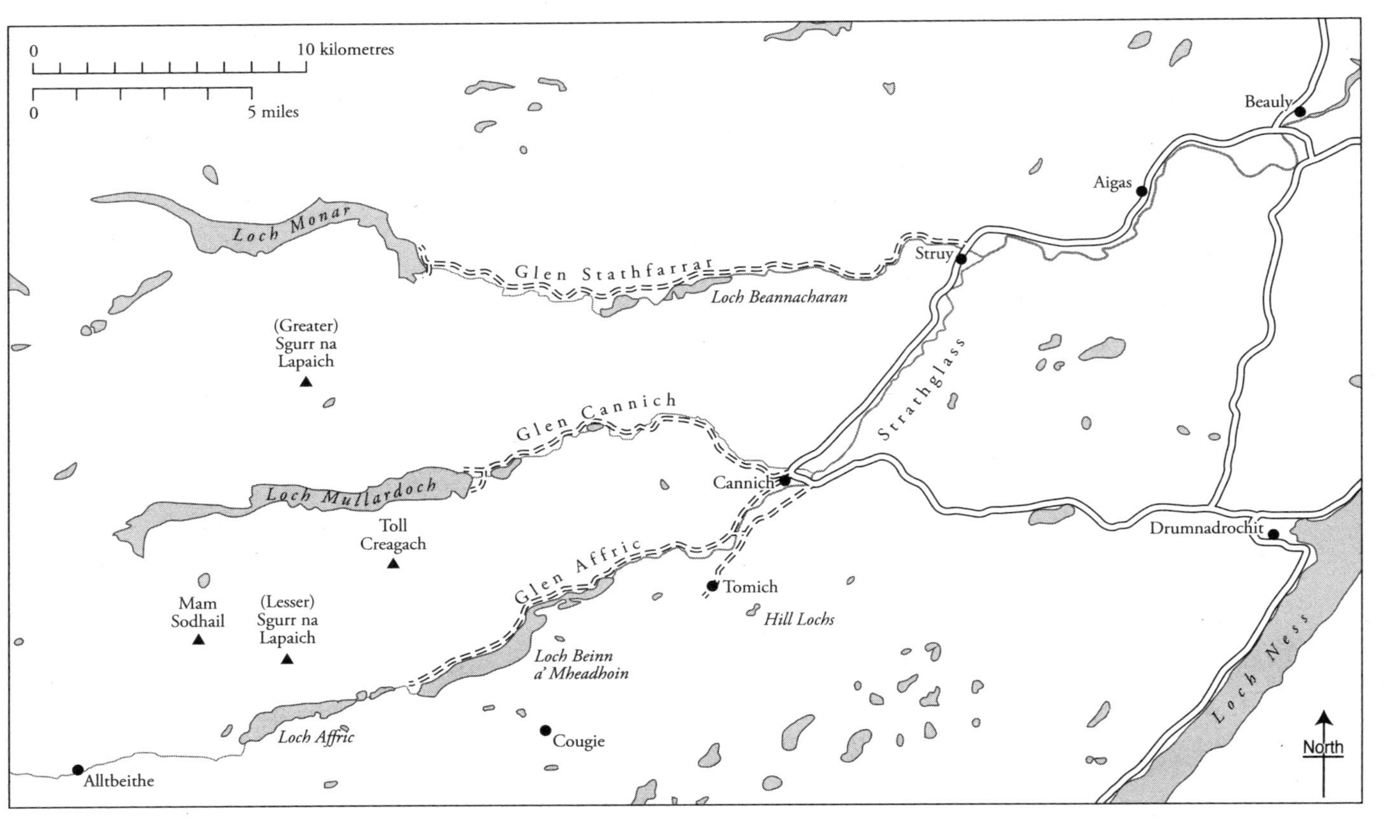

Strathglass and glens Affric, Cannich and Strathfarrar

1

There's an email from Tim.

> It's been very wet in the glen over the past few weeks and now serious flooding. My cattle got trapped on a very small island and I had to swim out to them with a bale of hay and lead them swimming back to dry land – very cold! If winters continue in this vein I'm not sure how habitable parts of the highlands will be in 10 to 15 years' time.

All the same, I go.

There are flood warnings all the way north and water sluices over the road. Past Struy, where the River Glass swings close to the road, a sheet of water has swamped road, fields and riverbank, barring the way. I'm reluctant to drive through – how deep is it?

An approaching Land Rover and trailer churn slowly through the water, throwing up bow waves. The burly driver, a farmer by the look of him, comes over as I sit watching from the car. 'You'll get through,' he says. 'Keep to the crown of the road. Canny as you go.'

Cannily I go.

The well-known surroundings are transformed. Strathglass is a different country, the riverbanks broken and submerged and the strath inundated here and there. Trees stick up from pools like tropical rainforest, islets speckle lagoons where there was only dry land before and newly formed burns pouring down from the high ground swill across the road.

My temporary home for the next few nights is a caravan in Cannich village. Rain drums on the van roof overnight and, in the morning, it's raining still, though with lessened force. I was cold in bed – three degrees. No newspapers in the shop – they didn't get through – and no post. The overside road is closed and the news is that the road down to Drumnadrochit is flooded just before the village. The Beauly road could be blocked if it gets worse. There might be no way out. Marooned!

Tim takes me to meet Sheena, who farms cattle in the glen, and we stand at the gate in our wellies, in a welter of mud. Tim admits he didn't actually swim, though it was touch and go. He waded out breast high towards his stranded animals holding a heavy bale of hay above his head while two of his daughters stood at the water's edge in case of emergency. After a good deal of cajoling, wheedling, calling the cattle by their names (he named them after the girls at the forestry office, though the girls don't know that yet), the hungry heifers edged off dry land into the water and followed him back to safety. Keeping his feet was a problem and several times he was in danger of lift-off.

Tim asks Sheena if she's noticed an increase in flooding since she's farmed here. She reflects a little – no, the waters haven't risen higher over the last 15 years or so, but probably floods have been more frequent.

Tim says that, between November and December, it rained for 46 days. That's biblical. Forty days and forty nights and then Noah pushed out the ark. It hasn't come to that yet.

'I'm going on a castration course,' Sheena remarks casually, 'so that I know which bits to cut off.'

Oh. It makes you wince.

In the afternoon, I venture into Glen Cannich, where there are signs that the floodwaters are receding. The hills have disgorged themselves by now. A high tidemark of litter, branches, torn-up bracken and grass shows the extent of the flooding. Everything's still sopping wet. Big spreads of water fill the low ground and the swirling river brims under the causeway to Craskie – I shan't risk a crossing.

There's a dank mistiness in the air, a ghostly calm now that the wind has died and the rain almost stopped. Brightness comes and goes in this new world. Now and again the low sun edges through, gilds the snow-streaked hilltops and freshens all the colours of the earth – the birch groves, leafless and wine-dark, golden larch, conifer woodlands vivid green, swags of withered bracken brick-red on the hillsides. Old twisted birch stems coated with grey-green lichens dip their feet in unaccustomed pools. Then rain-mist closes the shutters again.

2

No caravan this time. Where shall I stay?

A potholed lane, a farm shed smelling of dung, a tall white house. A ship's bell hangs on a rope at the door. *Clangalang!*

Jane, plump, a bit short of breath (she's asthmatic), answers the bell. She and her husband Ian run their home, Comar Lodge, as a bed and breakfast and, yes, there's a bed for the night. This tower-like house at the end of a farm track was built in the 1700s. The stones in the porch wall are scored where Jacobite soldiers sharpened their dirks in the Forty-five rising.

From my room at the top, there's a view of meadow and riverbank where sometimes, says Ian, you will see an osprey fishing. Between twin beds, a cabinet opens to reveal a chamber pot decorated with green flowers, chipped on the rim. There's an old-fashioned dressing table which will do for a desk though the mirrors are off-putting. In a cupboard under the eaves are a bottle or two of wine but they're probably not meant for guests. Just stored.

Down the road in Cannich village is the Slater's Arms, where Jimmac stands behind the bar. Jimmac, a gruff burly man, *was* a slater until he came down from the rooftops to pull pints. Business is brisk. I meet Mike, a freelance trucker taking a fortnight off from the road, who says he's trying to get fit with a bit of biking, a bit of walking and maybe some fishing. (You get fit fishing?) Also he's reconnoitring Strathglass to see if he can settle here and make a home. He lives in Dunfermline.

> The king sits in Dunfermline toun
> Drinking the bluid-red wine

Across the road is the Glen Affric Hotel. No, the Glen Affric Hot-l – an 'e' has dropped off.

Dimmed are the bright lights of yore. All's dark in the hotel except for a chink of light under a door. Inside the poky bar, silent, bare, uncarpeted, a solitary customer sits at a plain table with a pint in front of him, talking to a young (youngish) woman behind the tiny corner bar. She has dark hair with a hint of auburn in it. On the wall behind her is a gantry holding only three upturned bottles, though there's space for five.

I ask for a malt whisky. There's no malt. She answers cheerily, 'You can have Whyte and Mackay or Whyte and Mackay or Whyte and Mackay.' Three bottles. No malt, but it will serve.

Louise smiles at adversity.

Frank, her customer, runs a fire station in Birmingham and spends his two weeks off in eight in a cottage he bought just out of Cannich. He tells me of his 90-year-old neighbour, Old Duncan. 'You should speak to him. He's got lots of stories about the old days. He's writing a book about it.'

In comes Brian, a young Jamaican. Brian Chisholm – he's researching his roots in Affric, which is Chisholm country. What will he find? A Chisholm from Affric who came to the sugar island as a planter? A slave girl as his several-greats-grandmother?

Brian, while here, has set up an art gallery in a wing of the hotel where the dining room was. The room has been stripped and is eerie. Two bare bulbs cast a pale glow in the barn-like interior, which smells of damp. On the walls hangs an eclectic (to be polite) mix of pictures in different sizes and styles, most of them gaudy. But in one corner is something special, a small group of icons, as in an Orthodox church – meek virgins, adoring saints, babes wise beyond their years, all crowned in golden glories. Inclined heads, tapered fingers, arcane meanings. Not sentimental images for the tourists but the real thing, made by a nun who lives in Cannich.

Icons in Affric! Wonder of wonders.

In the garden seen from the bedroom window at Comar is a summer house, a gazebo with a table and weathered seats inside – a place to work, maybe, when the weather's warm. Beyond the fence there's a field dotted with browsing sheep, then a line of bare trees with a glimpse of the river, broad and rippling, and a ridge of forested hill hazy in the weak March sunshine.

Breakfast is set on the big table in a room furnished with antique oriental pieces. Ian was brought up in India, where his father was a planter. It's part dining room, part kitchen. Ian speaks from the Aga.

I ask about the icons.

'Sister Petra Clare,' says Ian. He says she's renowned far and wide for her work and gets orders for icons from across continents.

Sister Petra Clare lives at Marydale, the Catholic church in the pine trees across the road from the Cannich caravan park, where she offers a retreat to the faithful which Ian describes as 'gently commercial'. She may be seen walking down the street with hiking boots under her ample skirts.

(Some days later I do see her in the street – a large lady in flowing white from head to toe. Below her skirts, she's wearing – this I notice – thick socks and heavy shoes, not hiking boots this day. She proceeds in a stately fashion past the shop, billowing like a ship under sail. Should I say hello? But the moment is lost. She walks on with a wan smile on her pale face.)

As for the hotel, Ian thinks it's a hopeless case and it probably never made money, except for a brief interlude when the dams were building. Between the wars when it was a modest country hotel, it was favoured by the gentry who came to fish for salmon or trout or stalk the red deer. They dressed for dinner.

In those days as a simple country hotel, an unpretentious two-storey stone-built affair with an inviting air, it had a welcome for travellers. Then it got beyond itself. At the height of the dam-building boom, a wing was added in a 1930s ocean-liner style with a rounded facade and large metal-framed windows, brightly washed in white or cream. It was a mistake – the good times would never last.

Ian says Louise bought it on an impulse. She inherited money, arrived in Strathglass and fell in love with it and that was that. Gradually the paint began to peel, the window frames rusted and the hotel decayed.

I tell Ian that when Catherine and I spent a night at the Glen Affric Hotel years ago on the eve of our trek through Affric and Kintail it was a welcoming place, with lively company at the bar and in the dining room. There was warmth and chatter. We saw it at its best and remember it fondly.

3

There's no answer from Sister's quarters at Marydale Church, a grey stone building with a short steeple like a pencil stump. Maybe she's out or praying or singing the office or sleeping – she'll rise early for devotions.

The heavy church door swings open. In the porch is a small stone pyx with an inch of water in the hollow and a brass plate telling that it came from the ruins of a church built by the chief of the Chisholms to celebrate his conversion to Catholicism in 1660. A newel staircase winds up to the gallery and a heavy bell-rope knotted round an iron ring dangles from a trapdoor in the ceiling. Sister Petra Clare yanks on it to summon her flock to mass?

According to a notice, this is the church of Our Lady and St Bean and associated with it is the Sancti Angeli skete. Skete? A word not in my dictionary. There's an explanation on the wall: 'Sketes are small monastic houses and hermitages devoted to solitude and the community life. Sancti Angeli skete comes under the direction of the Abbot of Pluscarden. The Latin ritual is observed.' There's more – this, not addressed to me: 'Have you ever thought of becoming a nun?'

A framed document at the door relates history. Marydale parish is, or was in the 1930s when the document was put up, a swathe of land stretching from Drumnadrochit pier on Loch Ness to Benula in the north, a place now inundated by the Mullardoch dam, and far into Glen Affric in the west. The Marydale priest pre-war had a lot of ground to cover. Would he have had a car? A pony, a pushbike at least?

Inside, the church is plain, not ancient but bright and airy, simple and seemly. The ceiling, vaulted like the rib-work of an upturned boat, is coloured sky blue and dotted with stars. There's a plaster statuette of the virgin in pale robe, and Stations of the Cross along the wainscotted walls.

I venture up the corkscrew staircase (tucking in elbows in case of knocks) to reach the gallery. There are icons and unlit candles in red glasses on the front shelf and sheets of crabbed notation, angular dots hopping across the page – Gregorian chant, a mystery to me.

Back in the open air again I notice the date 1866 picked out in gold lettering on an antique black-painted ronepipe. The church, now almost a century and a half old, has a tidy, well-kept look, as you'd expect of a building renovated and maintained by Historic Scotland – and happily, still functioning as built, still a working church. Historic Scotland is mostly about ruins.

4

Gl-- Affric Hot-l.

More letters are missing.

A window's broken. But the door's ajar and Louise is at home.

Louise appears in a padded jacket and ushers me in. It's cold inside. A large log cut from the trunk of a tree is an island in the centre of the lobby floor. There's a ruck of unopened letters scattered on a side table. Bills, perhaps? Louise says the electricity has been cut off.

She takes me into the lounge where I sit on a distressed sofa beside a broken-tiled fireplace, circa 1950s, with the ashes of a dead fire in the grate. Two small curly-haired dogs rush at me barking and one leaps up and thrusts himself under my elbow.

She tells me she bought the hotel with money her mother left her when she died and at first she considered running it jointly with a local man who wanted to offer accommodation to his fishing clients. But his plans didn't accord with her freewheeling vision, which tended more towards a community of souls than a commercial undertaking, and he pulled out. Louise admits that the hotel has been 'a bit catastrophic'.

But she seems remarkably untroubled. The money's gone but the magic lingers on. A woman who phoned asking for payment of a bill broke off in the middle of the call to say she could hear birdsong. Louise held her mobile to the open window so that she could listen. 'Birds, trees – I just love it here,' she says.

Lying open on the table is a leather-bound book like an old-fashioned ledger, the pages covered in neat handwriting. 'I write down my thoughts in this book,' she says.

Might I read her thoughts? A key to her soul? I'm too diffident to ask so Louise remains an enigma.

5

I want to talk to a deerstalker.

'John MacLennan's your man,' says Ian. 'My neighbour.'

So I go down the lane and cross the road to John's bungalow on the hillside above Comar Lodge, where we sit outside in the pale sunshine.

John MacLennan has been stalking man and boy on the West Affric hills, hard country many miles away at the far end of the glen. According to the local custom he's Johnny Affric. His father Duncan, in whose footsteps he follows, was Dunky Affric (and John's wife is Cathy Affric). Billy MacLennan, his cousin, is the local builder and stalker at Fasnakyle but Billy's not an Affric – he's Billy Charm after his dad, who was called the Blue Charm. Strange name.

John's a thickset man, sturdy and deeply bronzed. He wears a deerstalker hat, green jersey with shoulder pads and wellies – he's been gardening. Cathy appears with a tray of coffee, shortbread, sponge cake and scones warm from the oven. This is a treat. She's famous along the glen for her baking.

West Affric, once a private estate, now belongs to the National Trust for Scotland which bans stalking for sport on its land. There's a twist to this. The trust needed to keep deer numbers down to encourage the ancient pinewood to regenerate and the group of sportsmen who used to shoot there volunteered to do the culling for them. So the trust kept its hands clean, the syndicate continued to stalk and John kept his job.

John attended the discussion when they all sat round the table and the deal was struck – somewhat uneasily on the part of the trust. He was amused to hear the trust's man grudgingly admit, 'I suppose the stalking's all right so long as you don't *enjoy* it.' My question is this: can I go out on the hill with them? Not to shoot – just to watch, as an innocent observer.

John gives me a hard look. 'How fit are you?' he asks. I must have passed muster. 'Phone me in August,' he says.

6

Cannich. The caravan park again.

I settle down to watch an old TV series, *Weir's Way*. I've been given the box set of DVDs.

Tom Weir, mountaineer, writer and broadcaster, came to Glen Affric to make the series 30 years or more ago but this is the first time I've had a chance to watch it.

As the film opens, he strides down the back road above the still-functioning hotel at Cannich, in breeches and a bobble hat, with an old-fashioned sloppy rucksack on his back – a wee man with stocky legs and a wee round face and a blob of a nose. He looks over Cannich village as it was then in the early '70s. The ground is bare beyond the shinty park, where there are bungalows now. This had been the site of a hutted encampment where 2,000 hydro workers lived when the dams in Glen Affric and Glen Cannich were being built.

He stands on top of the Affric dam in a woody gorge (relatively secluded, unlike the dams at Mullardoch and Monar), explaining that at first it was planned to flood the whole glen, converting Loch Beinn a'Mheadhoin and Loch Affric into a single great loch, swamping the stretch of river that links them, along with picturesque stands of Caledonian woodland, and submerging Affric Lodge and the keeper's house next to it. Common sense prevailed, luckily.

It's winter. He skips down snow-covered steps, followed less confidently by a dark-bearded man in a kilt – Finlay Macrae, then district officer for the Forestry Commission with Glen Affric in his beat. A visionary, a lover of the old trees, Finlay Macrae is a legend among foresters yet.

Tom meets the MacLennan brothers, Donald and Duncan, both tall and trim and in their 60s. Duncan, stalker John's father, now in his 90s – the Old Duncan I heard of at the hotel – does most of the talking. He's been a stalker, a forest ranger and a shepherd in his time and now has been writing his reminiscences.

Donald, also in his 90s, was a great fisherman in his day. People would ask him what fly he used. 'Och, just the blue charm,' he'd say, thus acquiring a nickname. He became 'the Blue Charm' or just 'the Charm'.

'What do you do on holiday?' asks Tom.

'A bit of fishing, a bit of shooting,' the Charm replies. Work or play.

Tom meets Duncan's wife and her younger son, another Duncan. Young Duncan, a bright lad, ruddy-faced and just out of his teens, says he doesn't fancy a desk job in town. Affric is where he wants to be, working in the open like his dad and his uncle. (Now he takes clients fishing on the loch. He has driven the school bus and, on occasion, he pulls pints in the pub.)

Tom Weir climbed on Everest before Hillary and Tenzing got to the top. In a postscript to the film, shortly before his death, when he's aged and feebler, he's asked if he has any regrets. 'I wish I was young again,' he says. A wistful note to end the film.

7

At the Spar shop, Cannich.

Here comes the Charm in deerstalker hat, upright on a yellow bike, pedalling in stately fashion down the road past the hotel.

He dismounts to buy milk and a loaf, a tall figure, erect, elderly, white moustached. I say hello and we talk a bit.

'Blethering again,' says a man in passing.

The Charm remembers Tom Weir in Affric. He showed him an eagle's nest and he admired the wee man's neat footwork on rock.

Blethering . . . For no reason at all, he starts to reminisce about the war and how he was captured at St Valery, fighting with the Highland Division in the rearguard on the way to Dunkirk. It rankles still that they were left behind. How the Germans walked their prisoners all the way to Poland, where he worked in a coal mine deep underground for two years. After that, they were marched back again, on the road from January to March, their progress marked by a line of turds in the snow, mile after mile.

As I leave the shop with the newspapers under my arm there's no sign of life at the sad hotel across the road. Nor at the distressed cottage in a field round the corner with sagging tin roof and flaking walls. It looks derelict but someone lives there and in the small caravan parked beside it all the same. He's called Geordie. His rag-fleeced sheep crop the grass around the cottage and the neighbours complain when they stray beyond. Gardens are sacrosanct.

Further on, past the shinty park, are the modern bungalows of 'Little England', an unofficial name where, no doubt, few of the residents speak with a good Scots accent. Not that it matters – incomers or not, we're all Jock Tamson's bairns, aren't we? Among the pine trees stands Marydale Church and Sister Petra Clare's solitary quarters, silent and still, peaceful as should be.

A puddly road leads to the caravans and my temporary quarters. I turn in, thinking that this place begins to feel like home. I could live here – well, for a little while at least. On the other hand, I'm not country and I suspect I'd find it hard to adjust. I wave to Matt who runs the site with amiable efficiency. An incomer from the south, he has seamlessly integrated into the community – obviously no problem for him. Little England? Pah!

8

I find Finlay Macrae at home in Dingwall.

It's 30 years after his meeting with Tom Weir in Affric. The inky beard is turning to grey. Tweed breeches knotted above sturdy calves. On the table lies a box with a set of bagpipes – he's a great piper. Affric pinewood has echoed to his tunes. When a new forestry office was to be built at Dingwall, he had the plans changed so there was room in the corridor for him to pace up and down while he practised.

A Skye man, Finlay was reluctant to leave the west coast when his job took him to Easter Ross. 'The bottom fell out of my world,' he says. But that was before he found Glen Affric. 'When I first saw Affric, the colour was on the birch and it was a wonderland.'

Finlay became a conservationist when it wasn't orthodox forestry to protect the Caledonian pinewoods.

He got to know the wildlife.

> Birds you get in Affric are the pinewood specialists, the caper [capercaillie], the crested tit, Scottish crossbill. The wryneck has been seen. Also associated waders, the red and black-throated diver, the osprey. Siskin and redpoll, they all add to the variety. And the moorland birds, greenshank, golden plover, the dotterel and the ptarmigan, both of which are found only above two thousand feet. The ring ouzel can be heard.
>
> The two best times to see Affric are in May with a little snow on the tops and fresh growth on the birch shading into the deep green of the pine, and in autumn when all the colours are showing. In the days before good communications I would just disappear into the forest.

Finlay tells me that once when he and a colleague had taken a boat up Loch Mullardoch and were walking along the rough ground on the south side, they came on a set of bare bones bleached white – the skeleton of a horse picked clean. When he told this to an old forester later, the man said, 'That would be Jimmy.' Those were the days when horses did the heavy hauling. The forester was working with Jimmy the Clydesdale when the horse slipped and broke a leg. They had to leave him lying and next morning they went back and shot him.

9

'You've come at the right time,' says Sister Petra Clare. 'I've just put the kettle on.'

A place is laid on the plain deal table, with a water jug and a glass. Sister lives frugally. We have coffee and she offers dry bread from a bowl.

Her face is pale, the skin translucent and a little waxy like alabaster, which suggests too much time spent indoors. A web of tiny wrinkles fans from the corners of her eyes when she smiles. A girlish smile. She wears a light blue top over a white smock. Under the skirts, I notice thick grey socks and trainers.

Propped against the wall is a large icon of the virgin and child against a background of gold lustre. Bare toes peep from under her purple robe and her hands are open as though offering the child for adoration as he floats free before her breast. The Madonna's nose is long and thin, with a bump in it. (I think of the poet Edith Sitwell, pictured in the biography I'm reading.) Under the straight line of her eyebrows, her eyes are brown.

Brown eyes? Do we know this? Is it biblical?

'Well,' says Sister, 'brown eyes seem to be right for the Middle East. But let's be honest, brown or blue, who knows?'

She invites me to see her workroom. This is a privilege since it's in the quarters reserved for female retreat and normally out of bounds to men.

On a bench, laid out like an alchemist's stall, is her collection of pigments in bottles and boxes containing brightly coloured powders, some ground from rock or clay, others reduced from metals and many scarce and difficult to get – in some cases because of health and safety regulations. One box contains a powder of viridian brightness called Moscow green, precious because it's no longer to be had.

Next door is her work in progress – a series of panels commissioned to celebrate the return of the Carmelite order to Britain after many years in exile. Under a golden sky, a mitred ecclesiastical figure – the patriarch of Jerusalem – sits on a throne with a tip of crimson cushion peeping from under his bottom. He's presenting a scroll to the leader of the newly founded order of Carmelite monks who kneels at his feet.

The patriarch wears a white gown embroidered with pale blue crosses, while the Carmelite is more humbly dressed in a woolly garment hooped bee-like in bands of white and brown. This two-tone fashion, says Sister, caused a stir. The Carmelites were mocked as the 'pied' brotherhood – pied as in magpies and other birds of variegated plumage – as a result of which they changed into habits in a less flamboyant style. Also in the frame is the prophet Elijah, by virtue of the time he spent as a hermit on Mount Carmel, and a number of brothers busy at various tasks. Some chop logs for firewood, one carries freshly baked loaves from the oven, another washes his pied habit in a tub and yet another scans an illustrated text. A group of monks appears to be just gossiping, passing the time of day.

Sister explains that the Carmelites owe their origin to the decision of certain crusading knights to opt out of their mission to kill infidels, seeking salvation instead on Mount Carmel, Elijah's former retreat in the Holy Land. 'I think of them as the first conscientious objectors,' she says. 'I'm not sure whether it was the third or fourth crusade. The third was Richard the Lionheart. The fourth was the sack of Constantinople – if so, they were well out of it.'

Every year Byzantium renews itself in Marydale, a little. Here Sister Petra Clare runs a class in icon making ('You don't call it painting,' she explains. 'Technically, you *write* an icon.')

She extends an invitation: 'Come and see us.' So I shall.

10

Marydale, autumn.

How to write an icon. Class starts in the kitchen with a reading from a book on the veneration of icons as established by the Council of Nicaea (now Iznik in Turkey) in the year 787. In spite of the dry language, the council appears to have been a stormy affair – lots of long beards wagging. 'It got quite venomous,' she says. 'Rather like prime minister's question time in parliament. They were really going at it.'

We watch a slide show of icons, with commentary by Sister, who draws attention to an image of James and Peter tumbling in space, weightless like astronauts, Peter head over heels: 'Just look at the arm and leg movement.' Andrew in swirling cloak: 'The garments point up to the head of the saint like a gentle candle flame, St Andrew inspired by the holy spirit.' Christ in glory framed or, rather, bracketed by Elijah and Moses: 'See how their forms echo the oreole.' And: 'See how Christ's feet are never planted but seem to float. The feet become irrelevant to the body weight.'

In such ecstatic freefall, feet can be fun. 'I always think humour comes out in the feet. You can imagine little dialogues going on between them.'

Class takes place in a small bare hall adjoining the church where work progresses at tables strewn with papers and pencils, tracings and sketches. Sister moves round each student, nodding approval or giving advice:

> Never start without thinking of the form . . . Work out from the energy lines . . . Get the proportions right and you find where the energies are, then you can fire away . . . Iconography is like Gregorian chant – there are things you don't grasp until you've practised it again and again.

Four students, all male, three of them priests and none of them young, are seated at the tables. Brian, an Anglican priest in his 60s from Loughborough, attends every year. He says he can't draw and traces every line, which Sister rather disapproves of. David is clearly more accomplished – he's meticulously outlining a Christ figure on squared paper. He says he has drawn and painted for more than 40 years, is a deacon in the Birmingham diocese and would have trained for the priesthood if he hadn't been married. Doctoring was his profession until he retired after a heart attack. Aonghas, small and dark, is a priest in Dublin. Michael, too, is a priest, formerly in the Glasgow housing estate of Drumchapel but now living and working in the north of Scotland. He wears a small silver cross on his jumper.

At midday pencils are laid aside and we cross to the church and climb to the gallery, ducking heads on the twisting stair, where the five of us make a crowd. In the gallery, candles illuminate several small icons each the size of a postcard.

Sister gives a short reading, touches a finger on the keyboard in front of her to find a note and waveringly chants the first phrase, followed by Michael's ringing baritone and rather feebly by the others. The text seems to be a dialogue with God, a series of alternating couplets seeking protection from, and vengeance on, the enemy. *Ding them doon!* We shuffle to our feet and sit again at intervals between psalms, with periods of silence for contemplation and prayer.

A short break outdoors in the sunshine follows, terminated by Sister vigorously ringing a large handbell as a summons to lunch.

Lunch at Marydale is a silent feast. We do not talk. Under a big cross on the dining-room wall, the table is set with thick crockery plates and bowls decorated with a gilt cross, upturned glasses and cutlery laid on napkins. There's a jug of water and cartons of apple and orange juice. After a short reading and a prayer, Sister leads us in line into the kitchen, where she ladles herself lentil soup from the pot, thick and brown, and we follow. We cut hunks of brown bread from a loaf on the sideboard, take a lump of cheese, a spoonful of pâté and an apple, banana or peach from the fruit bowl.

Once all are seated, Sister switches on an old tape machine on the windowsill and out booms an ecclesiastical voice reverberating in some church or perhaps cathedral, delivering a homily on the meaning (or, rather, the five meanings) of Lent – a journey, an offering, a fasting, a forgiving . . . and the fifth? I forget the fifth. But I recall the joke – you can eat steak every day including Friday, says the bishop on tape, and still be more forgiving than if you fast on lentils. A recorded titter ripples round the congregation and we chuckle too as we spoon our lentil soup.

From my seat at the end of the table, I look out through the window at a tree-covered hillside, a sky puffy with white clouds and, closer at hand, a woman cultivating the monastic garden, an appropriately life-enhancing (and biblical) activity.

11

Class is coming to its end. David has finished his icon, a grave greybeard St Nicholas with a pattern of crosses on his dress. Michael adds the last touches to the picture on his easel. Brian pores over a notebook. Sister sits with Aonghas, who's rubbing out bits of his pencil work, correcting the line.

'You missed the monks,' says Patricia when I return later to say goodbye. Patricia, from Nanaimo on Vancouver Island, is in retreat at the Marydale skete.

If only I'd known . . . This morning, I've been in Glen Affric and found the car park at the top of the glen thronged. Milling around three white minivans was more than a score of men of all ages, dressed in jeans or leather jerkins or tweed jackets, chattering and laughing. Somehow they didn't look like your average tourists. Who could they be? Monks from Pluscarden Abbey, as I learned later.

Once a year they break free of the cloisters and they'd called at Marydale for the midday office. They sang with gusto – 30 male voices raised in praise. The rafters rang.

Sister says they arrived out of the blue. She thought they might have left a message warning of their visit but she hadn't checked her emails. She's not very practical that way, which figures. Nuns are unworldly – right?

12

Breakfast at Comar Lodge, Ian at the Aga with the frying pan in his hand ('One egg or two?').

Where's a good short walk in the neighbourhood? – 'The Hill Lochs,' says he. 'Start at Tomich.'

Tomich, three miles upstream from Cannich, looks a village out of place and time. It's a row of neat stone cottages all built to the same pattern, with latticed attic windows and flower baskets at the doors. There's more to it than that, but not much. These doll's-house cottages survive more or less as built, though gentrified now, along with a small hotel and a tiny Post Office – a wooden chalet painted blue with fretwork eaves, open for business six hours a week. At the roadside stands a memorial drinking trough, with fountain (now dry) in a shell-like recess from which, in another climate, I fancy Venus might emerge naked. But it's springtime in Tomich with a frost on the ground and a nip in the air.

The fountain bears medallion portraits of the Tweedmouths, lord and lady, in low relief. All the land for miles around belonged to the Tweedmouths and Tomich was their model village.

Tall iron ornamental gates stand permanently open at a wonky angle. At the top of the drive a stable block, unseen from the road, comes suddenly into view. This is no ordinary stable block but a rather grand affair, a handsome steading in pink stone designed to impress, with a clock tower above the archway. It has been converted into tourist accommodation but this is the slack season and there's no one about except for a man in a tractor digging in the field.

Not far from this elegant stable block is a villa in the same pink sandstone, which used to be the home farm for the Guisachan Estate in the Tweedmouths' day. Here lives Donald Fraser, once a farmer in a gentlemanly sort of way, amateur sailor and owner of the remains of the estate.

The track leads up past the stable block to open moorland, a heather-darkened landscape of hollows and hillocks. Ahead there's a glint of water – Loch a'Ghreidlein, the first of the Hill Lochs. A low hill above it is topped by what might be, as seen from a distance, a slender obelisk, a needle outlined against the sky. In spite of its name, Beinn Mhor (Big Hill), it is only 401 metres high but the climb is stiff enough to cause me to break sweat. At the top, I find the heather burned off and green shoots already poking through the tangle of charred stems. They crunch pleasantly underfoot.

The monument turns out to be a Celtic cross engraved with the names Edward, Lord Tweedmouth (died 1909) and Fanny, his lady (1904), erected – it says – by the grateful tenants of Guisachan Estate. (Grateful for what?)

Tweedmouth? It sounds familiar. But I'm thinking John Buchan of *The Thirty-Nine Steps* and other 'shockers' as he called them, later a grand public servant and consequently Lord Tweedsmuir. Tweedmouth was obviously quite another fellow.

There are five Hill Lochs but from the top of Beinn Mhor I see only two. The three smallest lochans in the chain are hidden by a shoulder of the hill and by dips and rises in the land below. This is a Lakeland in miniature, the lochs diminishing in size to the smallest only 30 or 40 metres across. Even that pool has a name – Loch na Gobhlaig. Southwards from my viewpoint lies a swathe of dark conifer woodland with pale patches of larch showing through. In the days of the Tweedmouths, this was open moorland. Towards the west rises the knobbly brow and steep scarp of the little hill Beinn nan Sparra (Hill of the Spars), shaggy with scattered pine trees. A string of pylons punctuates the middle distance. In the far west, the high hills of Affric and Kintail stretch across the horizon streaked with snow. Through half-closed eyes – I squint against the wind – they have the look of distant Alps.

It's chilly, winter barely gone. I look around briefly, take it all in, then hasten down.

Perched over the water's edge at Loch a'Ghreidlein is a wooden boathouse and, close by it, a beehive-shaped cairn of grouted stones blotched with golden lichens, 'in memory of a lover of this countryside' – a fisherman no doubt. At the foot of the cairn is the bone of a small animal, picked clean by hoodie crow or some hook-billed bird.

In the shallows further round the lochan, just under the surface, there lurks ghostly debris – blanched branches and tree stumps embedded in the peat. No trees grow round the Hill Lochs now.

13

In the grocer's shop in Cannich, I have bought a small yellow-covered booklet called *Guisachan, a History* in which Donald Fraser tells the story of the Tweedmouths and their association with this part of the world.

The first Lord Tweedmouth, plain Edward Dudley Coutts Marjoribanks before ennoblement, was a wealthy industrialist and keen country sportsman who bought the Guisachan Estate in the mid 19th century for its 20,000 acres of shooting. He is said to have got it cut-price when he finessed the owner out of a 300-year-old inheritance.

The owner held a dinner party at which Marjoribanks was a guest. Wine and spirits flowed. In the course of the feast, the host grumbled that he'd 'sell Guisachan tomorrow' if anyone offered £60,000 – £52,000 according to another version of the tale – for it. 'Done!' cried Marjoribanks from the far end of the table. When the owner, sobered in the light of morning, tried to withdraw the offer, Marjoribanks held him to it. A gentleman's word was his bond in the etiquette of the day.

In due course the first Tweedmouth, father of Edward on the monument, cleared his tenants from their scattered drystone, mud-floored huts and settled them at Tomich in newly built estate houses where, in spite of all the latest Victorian mod cons, the uprooted tenants (grateful as maybe) apparently never felt at home. It's said they made regular pilgrimage to gaze tearfully on their old forsaken cabins.

14

Donald Fraser opens the door. 'We usually sit in the kitchen,' he says, leading the way.

An appetising aroma of baking greets us there – Donald's wife Sue is baking cakes and offers me one straight from the oven. Mmm.

Donald's livelihood used to be farming, but he gave that up years ago. He says that farming cattle at Guisachan didn't appeal to him and, when the bottom fell out of the beef market in the 1980s, he sold the herd to concentrate on the holiday trade, building chalets behind the trees and converting the nearby stable block and farm steading into cottages for tourists.

Now he's about to set out on a great adventure. Outside, a marquee has been set up on the lawn. Their daughter is to be married on Saturday, 200 guests are invited, and then Donald is off to sea. 'I'm a serious sailor,' says he.

Donald, fortyish, sturdy, is going to sail round the world in a boat he built himself in a shed. He built the shed too. A friend from the village will crew her. She's already made her maiden voyage via the Bay of Biscay to the Med, where Donald will board her for the voyage.

He learned to sail dinghies at school and, when he progressed to Sandhurst and a career as an army officer, boats came into that too. He was attached to a team maintaining and sailing yachts for the armed services, based at a diving school on the Solent. Why would the army need yachts? 'Character building,' he says, 'part of the training.'

They looked after themselves well. There was the odd trip to Cherburg to bring back a few crates of duty-free French wine – all part of the training, of course.

His boat is a 39-foot steel-hulled vessel named *Spirit of Affric*. A naval architect drew up the plans and the steel plates were cut to size by computer and trucked up to Tomich where he put them together, learning the craft of boatbuilding as he went along. The timberwork and fittings were cut from larch and oak trees felled at Guisachan. So a piece of Affric sails the seven seas.

15

I take the potholed woodland road beyond Tomich that leads to a car park in the trees with a signpost pointing to Plodda Falls, a local beauty spot. A slender spout of water gushes a hundred feet into black pools. The track ends at a cliff edge where a narrow iron lattice bridge spans a gorge. Now it goes nowhere since it's blocked by a railing but, in Tweedmouth days, it led to a network of adventurous paths on the far side. Downstream from the bridge, I walk through an avenue of handsome Douglas fir trees established long before the Forestry Commission appeared on the scene to engulf the ornamental trees with commercial conifers.

At length, the woodland opens out into a kind of distressed parkland marked by two ragged chestnut trees and, by the roadside, men are at work on old outbuildings with a picturesque little turret on top. A builder's van stands outside, planks are propped against the wall and through frameless windows comes the sound of hammering and sawing. Gentrification is in progress. The old estate stable is about to become a country residence.

A few hundred yards on, unexpectedly, I come on the last remains of the old Guisachan House, gaunt and ruinous in its dilapidation. A fence of rickety paling surrounds it and red signs – Danger, don't enter! – warn off inquisitive intruders. The roof's off, the windows are out, the walls all broken and crumbling. Door frames gape. Laths poke from broken plaster. Screes of broken masonry choke the interior and overhanging stones threaten to totter and fall. Small trees and shrubs have taken root in crevices in the masonry.

Where the main entrance was, formal steps lead up to a jagged gap in the facade. The bay windows from which house guests could survey the park are blank. And, at the back of the ruin, only an outline on the stonework shows where the orangery was.

It's a sad remnant. If the weather hadn't got to it first, the builders might now have been busy there too, hammering and sawing, converting the mansion into flats for incomers or holiday homes. But Guisachan is gone with the wind like Tara.

It has a footnote to fame of a sort. A slate tablet in the grass (no longer a lawn) dated 2002 records Guisachan as birthplace of the golden retriever. Here in 1868, as Donald Fraser recounts in his history of Guisachan, the first Tweedmouth mated a yellow wavy-coated retriever bought from a cobbler in Brighton with a Tweed water spaniel. Black retriever crosses, an Irish setter and even a bloodhound were involved in the line before the breed was established. Thus Guisachan House in its decay has become a place of pilgrimage for doggy folk.

A signposted walk leads to a higher level through Guisachan's former policy woods. Douglas firs abound, one snapped in a recent storm and measuring its length on the turf. Another, broken off long ago, stands bare and pitted by wood-boring insects. Here and there, there are big sequoias – Wellingtonias by another name – some still protected by rusted metal railings and, around them, the stumps of spruce and larch, planted thoughtlessly in the years of aggressive forestry and now felled to give the big trees room to recuperate.

Once the first Tweedmouth had acquired the estate, he set about improving the property. He built the mansion and its associated buildings – kennels, stables, laundry, brewery, meal mill – and the model village at Tomich including a school, plus the handsome farmhouse with its dairy and stable block.

He, and after him his son, held open house for celebrated guests. His daughter-in-law Fanny was a Spencer Churchill and her nephew Winston was an occasional house guest. Somewhere (not in Fraser's book) there's a photograph of the young Churchill standing beside a motor car outside the Guisachan carriage stable. He learned to drive there.

Earlier visitors included the artists Landseer and Millais. The Duke and Duchess of York, later George V and Queen Mary, came to stay and, while there, planted the pair of horse chestnut trees (still to be seen), along with a third planted by an Indian maharajah. Gladstone came and, sometime about 1890, planted three Douglas firs near Plodda – 'now a noticeable landmark towering above the surrounding Forestry Commission plantations', according to Donald Fraser. In the glory of his prime Gladstone would chop down mighty trees with his axe for sheer pleasure, sometimes watched admiringly by bonneted ladies, so he may have gazed enviously at some of the giants at Guisachan. But by then, in 1890, the old warrior was in his 80s and his tree-felling exploits were in the past.

Old photographs in Donald Fraser's booklet give a glimpse of life as it was at the big house. One shows a line of horses, dogs and humans, including Lord and Lady Tweedmouth, posed before the house, which dominates the scene like a stage set. This, according to the caption, was a shooting party, though there's no sign of guns. Tweedmouth, heavily bearded and clutching his wrists limply in a less than lordly fashion, is dressed casually for the sport in a swallow-tailed tweed coat. His lady wears a skirt to her ankles and a hat flat and wide as a pancake. Among various dogs, an ancestral golden retriever lies in front of his master looking leonine. Eight docile ponies are held by tweeded retainers in breeches – one with spats over his stockings – except for the figure dressed incongruously in a dark suit, collar and tie and a bowler hat, who is identified as Sandy Post – Sandy the postman. This is the outdoor party and you wonder what busy life existed invisibly behind the windows and 'downstairs' – the cook, the housekeeper, the footmen, the maidservants and skivvies and all.

Behind this gathering the many tall sash windows of the house are neatly curtained. There are stone balustrades at roof level, mansard attics in the roof, decorative ironwork on the ridges and a perfect forest of tall chimneypots. Another photo shows the house from a different angle with the carriage drive curving towards it and a tiny tree protected by a wire enclosure. This, says Donald's caption, is 'the newly-planted Wellingtonia'. He suggests the reader might compare it with the giant of today. Yet another picture shows a large domed orangery or greenhouse nestling at the back of the house, all trace of which is gone.

The second Lord Tweedmouth, besides his interests as a landed gentleman, had political ambitions. He became a Liberal MP, served as Chief Whip in Gladstone's last government and then as First Lord of the Admiralty when the Liberals returned to power early in the 20th century. He was said to be one of the finest shots in Britain and, according to Donald Fraser's text, 'was always ready to take himself off from dawn to dusk to a rewarding trout stream'. But after Fanny died, still young, in 1904, he retreated from Guisachan and sold it. With his departure, the big house began its gradual decline. Let out to a variety of shooting tenants who had no particular love for it, the house was sold on and, finally, the last owner took the roof off and it was left to decay.

There's a postscript. At Upper Glassburn, a bed and breakfast place where I like to stay, talk of Guisachan prompts landlord George to open a drawer and pull out a few sheets of paper – a schedule for the sale of Guisachan Estate at auction in London, dated July 1935.

Included in the sale were the mansion house ('23 miles distant from

Beauly station on the Highland Railway'), home farm, hotel, post office and shop, school and school house, sawmill, plus the village of Tomich with its 25 cottages (householders all named in the sale document) and sundry lodges and other dwellings in the neighbourhood – the tenants' homes in Tomich were to be bought and sold in Berkeley Square without a by-your-leave like agricultural implements in a farm roup.

Also thrown in are the deer forest, the grouse moor and the fishing rights, making a grand total of 7,242 acres. The canny lawyer who bought all this in 1935 promptly got rid of the deer forest and sold the rest of the land to the Forestry Commission, which set about blanketing it with spruce and larch and pine, usually of foreign origin.

The bare details in the schedule give an insight into life in the grand country house – 15 bedrooms for residents, 16 bedrooms for servants, five bathrooms, 10 lavatories and WCs, four drawing rooms and a boudoir. There were stables for 20 horses and a garage for three cars – horses still being the principal mode of transport. Housemaids' sinks and coal bunkers were provided on every floor – I picture some skivvy digging into the bunker at the crack of dawn, filling the scuttles and lugging them along the corridors to the guest rooms in a trail of coal dust.

16

Walter on the phone – hard-of-hearing Walter. There's a shriek in the background. 'It's the parrot,' he says.

Did he say parrot? (My hearing's dodgy too.)

It *is* a parrot. Perched in its roomy cage, a bird with a hooked beak. Long John Silver comes to mind. Parrots are coloured like the rainbow, aren't they? But this one's drab. He makes a dart at the bars with fierce intent; he squalls and squawks with wordless fury.

Walter leads the way to his den where the bird is almost but not quite out of earshot. There's an occasional muffled volley from next door. Through the wide window are views of fields, woods and hill. The den is a mixture of ancient and modern, with a computer on the desk and other electronic gadgetry but also an African mask and carvings on the shelves and a flintlock musket with bayonet fixed hanging on the wall. Perhaps Walter was an old colonial with an interest in antique weaponry. But it seems not: 'They're just decoration'.

Walter is tall, heavily built, has bushy eyebrows, walks stiffly and eases himself into the swivel chair at the desk. He's a leader of the community with a gruff way of expressing forthright opinions – scorning, for example, all professional environmentalists and conservationists, which is what the talk turns to. All this twaddle about protecting birds of prey . . . Ask the locals, he says, the locals know best. Ask the stalkers and the gillies. But, because country folk don't write down their lifetime experiences, nobody listens to them and they're dismissed as having nothing to contribute to the debate.

Take pine martens, says Walter. (Pine martens are furry, bright-eyed, mean little killers, harried almost to extinction by gamekeepers but now legally protected and proliferating.) Walter's wife, bringing the tea tray, agrees. A pine marten took their neighbour's rabbits the other day and, before that, another neighbour lost all her chickens.

We talk of the woodlands, the Forestry Commission, and Trees for Life, an organisation with an outstation in Plodda woods whose members have been helping the commission to plant native trees. Trees for Life aims to combine an alternative philosophy (it's linked with the Findhorn Foundation) with practical work literally at ground level. Their director is Alan Featherstone. 'I call him Alan Featherbrain,' says Walter.

'You have to meet Stuart,' says Walter. 'I'll take you.'

We drive up a steep tree-shaded lane just before Tomich, past a derelict car, some builder's junk, an untidy pile of plastic bags and a stack of planks and arrive in a storybook.

There's a lawn with a winding path, a murmuring stream and a water-wheel, a well and a host of daffodils in flower. At the focus of view stands a tiny cottage with latticed peephole windows and a low oval doorway. It's a hobbit house out of Tolkien.

An elfin woman perched on top of a ladder is busy at some work under the eaves. Below her Stuart, equally short in stature, appears at the threshold with an invitation to come in. 'Mind your head,' he says – at five foot three he fits neatly within the door frame but anyone taller has to stoop. 'Tina,' he says, introducing the woman on the ladder, and we exchange vertical greetings.

The tiny low-ceilinged living-room-cum-kitchen is a surprise. It's cosy, snug as a nest, gleaming with polished wood, copper and chinaware, and there's hardly a straight line anywhere. A settle curves round an eccentric table – a piece of solid dark furniture fluted like the base of a cathedral pillar or the stump of some great forest tree – which it was. Stuart carved it by hand from the base of a cut-down yew.

It looks a dead weight, a brute to move, but not so. Yew, says Stuart, is so dense that it sinks in water but he hollowed it out and honeycombed it with miniature concealed drawers so that it glides on castors at a fingertip touch.

There are other curiosities. The fire in the hearth serves a double purpose, heating both the living room and also, by a curious sleight of hand, the stove in the adjacent kitchen area, where two shining copper hotplates serve as a poor man's Aga. The keyhole TV concealed behind panel doors pivots within the width of the wall to provide late-night viewing in the adjoining bedroom. Everywhere are inventive devices, all practical and most of them conceived of and crafted by Stuart. Before-and-after photographs show the stages in his conversion of the former derelict cottage and byre into this nursery-rhyme dwelling.

Stuart is a woodman by heart and by trade. His life has been spent working with timber, from tree-felling to carpentry. He once operated a sawmill in Australia. But he wears a hair shirt – working with hardwoods like oak or elm, the species of timber a craftsman prefers, triggers an irritating allergy due, he suspects, to some chemical in the wood. Softwoods like spruce and fir don't affect him in the same way but softwoods he disdains.

A narrow turning stair leads to Tina's bright bedroom under the attic roof. Halfway upstairs a door opens off the landing into the lavatory where the stately throne-like loo has been hollowed from the bole of another tree, a burr elm, beautifully figured. It's a joy to sit on. Perched there you may observe the garden through a small window (a loo with a view), meditate and listen to the birdsong. And from the adjoining shower cubicle you may step straight into the garden, robed if you wish, but, in any case, screened from view by the trees.

No one will pry. The cottage is sequestered, unseen, its very existence unsuspected from the road below.

One year later Stuart and I sit side by side on the settle with mugs of tea on the yew-tree table while Tina chops rhubarb in the galley kitchen. I feel like a character in a tale by Beatrix Potter – 'The Tale of Nutshell Cottage'.

Stuart's inventive mind is crammed with theories – in this case, a long and baroque fantasy concerning Rosslyn Chapel and the Templars and a tantalising biblical code (but not *The Da Vinci Code* – it was before that phenomenon) which Stuart credits implicitly: gospel truth. He pulls a book from the hand-made shelf, a work written by a former journalist on the *Washington Post*. Influenced by the theories of a maverick mathematician, the writer argued that predictions about future events could be found embedded in the Old Testament and may be decoded from the text by computer analysis of word and letter patterns. By this means, it can be shown that the Kennedy assassination, Hiroshima, the Holocaust, 9/11 and many more disasters were all foretold in scripture.

I listen with hooded eyes. If only we had known.

What horrors lie ahead? – and can we change the script before it's too late?

I don't ask. Better to turn the conversation to safer topics, like his life story – his spell as a cane-cutter in Australia, his time as a national serviceman in Korea calculating the position of enemy gun emplacements from flashes in the night or his experiences on holidays in peacetime Vietnam, charmed by the kindness and friendliness of the people. He fishes out the tourist snaps – the places he and Tina saw, the people they met and, especially, their waif of a translator, whose name they struggled to pronounce until she asked them to call her Tweet. 'Tweet's lovely,' he says.

And he talks about his inventions, like his proposed device for heating water by the sun. Serious physics is involved though the preparatory work has been practical and simple. With a nail, a stake and a length of string, he traced an outline of the sun's shifting shadow throughout the daylight hours, giving him the pattern for a parabolic mirror which, when polished and fixed in position, would concentrate the sun's rays on a water tank, thus causing the water to boil.

He's in full flight when there's a knock on the door. Chance visitors from Holland have arrived, a tall man and a gangly wife who saw Stuart's house on Dutch TV and have come here to see for themselves. They've come unannounced but Stuart breaks off to give them the guided tour, upstairs and down. They coo and ooh and aah at his cabinet of delights and leave happy at what they've seen.

'I'm not clever,' says Stuart. 'I just try harder. That's what Einstein said, by the way. But I'm not Einstein, I'm not much good at anything.' (This is not true.)

Will his sun heater work? Perhaps he should patent it? No. This will be his gift to mankind. And he adds, 'I'm trying to die penniless. I live simply. I don't need much. I can live on my pension. I can go to Vietnam – it doesn't cost the earth.'

He says any spare cash he gets helps to pay for small things for the people he meets in Vietnam, who have little. So, as I leave, my coins chink in the mug by the door.

17

Up before seven, I go outside for a breath of fresh air and walk among the pine trees at the caravan park. The ground is soft and mossy and scattered cones crackle under my feet. No one else stirs – it's Sunday and most of the vans are still unoccupied.

Sitting by the table at breakfast, I see cars arrive at the church across the road and people appear. I see Sister Petra Clare hurrying across the gravel to greet her flock, billowing in white.

I cycle by the river and stop at a little roadside cemetery. It's modern and not particularly picturesque. There's no church and never has been – no gravestones hoary with age. The broad River Affric swirls past under a high bank and a man up to his waist in the water is fishing. Not far beyond, where there's turbulence in the water, stands the Fasnakyle Power Station and, on the other side of the road, half hidden in the trees, is a substation festooned with power lines and beside it is the small stone villa at the top of a slope where a Mr Kwint, owner of a nearby estate, stays when he visits his land from his home in Holland. There's no other habitation except for a derelict but-and-ben, once home to Black Sandy (black because of his beard, not his nature).

I push open the iron gate and enter. Conifer and alder trees line three sides, with a trickle of burn, more of a ditch really, running over stones outside the fence. There are gravel paths and two or three neat rows of headstones in a grassy triangle, with gaps here and there and room for more. Most of the slabs are plain – some highly polished black granite. Some of the older stones are already dotted with lichens while a few of the more recent have pictures engraved on them – a deer on a hill and, on another, a shepherd and his dog ('partner of Sheena', it says).

Turnover seems to be slow – there can't be more than 30 graves in all, dating from the '70s to the present.

I read the names. Here lies Clement Lister Skelton (August 1919 to February 1979), 'actor and author'. What books, what stage? He left this world in confident assurance: 'My love, my love, we will all be merry in heaven.' The posy of roses above his grave is only slightly faded.

There's an Ivan Orr Toulmin-Rothe, forester – a strangely exotic name. And Wladislaw Rura, occupation unspecified, with an eagle and gilt crown cut into the stone at the top and two lines in Polish below, now hard to decipher. Tender inscriptions, banal enough, reach out bravely beyond the formulaic – innocent expressions of grief carved in stone.

Mary McKechnie, 'asleep amid the hills she loved, to awake in heaven', joined 13 years later by her husband 'who whilst walking in the hills lay down amongst them and fell asleep'. A cry for June Hamilton: 'O for the touch of a vanished hand and the sound of a voice that is still.' A quotation? – not one that I recognise.

Most touching of all are the reminders of young lives lost, such as the 24-year-old soldier of the Queen's Own Highlanders: 'May his sacrifice help to bring the peace and freedom for which he died' (forlorn hope). Saddest of all, the infant deaths – the child who died at Christmastime (a bambi on his stone), another, a 'darling infant son' (a twin) and 'our baby son . . . went to sleep'.

No one I knew lies here but I'm moved. I close the gate softly behind me.

18

Comar Lodge, five in the morning.

It's pitch dark, Ian and Jane still sleeping. I creep downstairs and walk gingerly down the lane by torchlight, startled by sounds of heavy breathing – unseen cattle in the field. Strong smell of dung and the warm gust of a beast's breath over the fence.

Headlights approach on the road and Dave the birdman pulls up in his Land Rover. He clears a space in the clutter and I climb aboard.

We head uphill from Cannich, turning off at a signpost indicating a chambered cairn. But old stones are for another day – we're off to witness a lek. Dave is the RSPB's man here and a lek is the dawn mating display of black grouse – cock birds facing up to their rivals and displaying in front of the females. (Black grouse are cousins of the more familiar red grouse and the now rare capercaillie, grandest bird of the forest.) Leks take place twice in the year, in spring and autumn. A brief flurry, says Dave, and then, soon after sunrise, the show's over.

The sky begins to lighten as we drive along a rough road through avenues of big trees, with a farmstead and a few old houses just visible at a bridge over the River Enrick. Twice, gates barring the road have to be opened. We reach open moorland where a slit of water known as Loch Comhnard glints in the half-light. Here we leave the vehicle and Dave sets off long striding through shrubby heather sprinkled with tufts of white bog cotton – a favourite feed for black grouse, he says. I find it hard to keep up. The slope is sore on thigh muscles and the pulse races.

We can't be far from the action. There's a faint burbling in the air like the noise of distant running waters but in fact it's the sound of blackcock in a state of agitation. Dave scans the ground ahead with binoculars and finds birds clustered on a distant grassy ridge. He counts 11 but they're too far away to be seen with clarity – a small congregation of black blobs in jerky movement.

Is this all? Did we rise early for this? Frankly, I'm disappointed. It's not David Attenborough.

Now the sun edges above the low, blue, distant hills and strands of cloud on the horizon are barred with red. Hanks of mist shroud Affric and the glens of Strathglass. A rising wind chills on the small eminence on which we stand and gloves, muffler and woolly hat are welcome.

Dave decides to move on, leading the way through a tangle of recently felled young trees. They're lodgepole pines of North American origin and, as such, unwelcome on RSPB territory. Crossing this tract of deadwood and tussocks pitted with bog pools is hard labour. Two red deer move across the skyline on the far side of the Enrick and then a couple of roe deer hinds bound across the felled trees just ahead of us, white rumps bobbing.

All the time Dave's on the lookout for birdlife of all kinds – lark, thrush, lapwing in baggy-winged flight down by the loch. We hear the call of the curlew and the chip-chip of the crossbill. Two greylag geese rise from the loch, circle and return. Dave says the pair remain all year round, nesting in the heather close to the water. He hopes they'll breed.

Driving back along the Enrick, casting an eye about, Dave stops, raises his binoculars. Hush! He's seen three black grouse, two males and a female, just yards away in the roadside vegetation. They're clear to the naked eye and, seen through binoculars, they leap in scale – the males large and glossy black with white under-feathers showing at their tails and bright red wattles above their eyes. One, speckled with white, is a young bird, probably a year old. One of the two males hops with fluttery bobs in the air, a foot or so off the ground, then pauses and stands casting haughty glances. His rival male lowers his head, stretches his neck and makes a running charge through the undergrowth. They square up to each other, jabbing and thrusting just short of making contact. Dave says there's seldom more to it than that, at most a few feathers will fly. Meanwhile the slender-necked, grey-brown female stands by patiently awaiting the outcome.

Dave is pleased to find them. He encouraged the farmer to graze his cattle here for a couple of months to promote the growth of a sward for the birds to feed on and here's evidence it has worked.

Another day, another early morning wait at the lane end. Dave's late. Five minutes, ten, fifteen . . . Cars go by, one two three, and a truck and then the farmer from down the lane who waves from his tractor. Otherwise the road is empty.

The old Land Rover appears at last and I hoist myself into the seat. Jenny the collie, who's been curled on the floor, rouses herself to lick me round the ear.

Again we bump along the Corrimony track to Loch Comhnard, where we tumble out and set foot on a heathery hill.

'Listen!' says Dave and he purses his lips and cheep-cheeps. Chip-chip comes back a faint call. 'Reed bunting,' says he.

Two dots curve above our heads: 'Meadow pipit chasing a cuckoo.' (Small brown birds in flight look much alike to me.) Then, 'Mistle thrush,' as another brown bird lands on the grass not far from where we stand. From uphill, where a big old rowan leans over a rocky cleft, comes an imperative cry: 'Chaffinch.' But even I know that.

Today we're looking for trees – seedling trees in trial plots planted by the RSPB with the long-term aim of improving the habitat for bird life, hence Dave's interest. The trees will provide shelter and food for several species but mainly black grouse. Here, on this hillock, the carpet of brown heather is sprinkled with green dots where infant pine trees are just beginning to poke above the vegetation.

A wooden stake has been driven into the ground in the centre of the plot. Dave attaches a tape measure to the stake then draws out the tape to precisely 5.6 metres. My job is to walk in a circle round the post like a horse in a meal mill, keeping the tape taut, while he hunkers down and notes the condition of each seedling tree within the defined circle, assessing its health and measuring its growth since the last inspection.

One specimen has a sickly yellowy look which indicates that it's severely parched. Dave blames a bone-dry April. 'Pathetic,' he says.

Dave's interest in the progress of his plants is more than botanical. Money comes into it. The trial plots are subsidised by grants and if too few saplings come away in a given period, the Forestry Commission will claim the money back. So far so good – Dave reckons that even the feeble specimen has made sufficient growth to count.

The next plot lies in a hollow. Dave, stricken: 'Oh my God, pine weevil. God, there's always something.' He finds a little curled-up caterpillar on a pine shoot, then the weevil itself, which he pinches between his fingers. He discovers no more so it's hardly an infestation. 'We may get away with it.' Then on second thoughts, dolefully: 'Maybe we'll have to spray after all.' Chemical sprays are not good news for conservationists.

All's well in a dell where the heather grows high and the pine plants are fresh and sturdy, flourishing in the shelter. 'Nice dry bank, sunny situation – just fine.' And 'Wow, look at that. Don't want to wax lyrical but that one is *away*.'

Everywhere there are wildflowers. Wood avens, globeflower, chickweed wintergreen, plenty of wood anemone and a little blue flower carried on slender stems springing from fleshy leaves – butterwort, the fly eater.

All around there's a promising growth of shrubby things. I prick my finger on a little broom-like shrub – 'Petty whin,' says Dave (petty for small). It's something I've never seen, or at least never noticed before, though Dave says there's quite a lot on this ground.

Down by a small burbling burn half hidden in a grassy dell, there's a spread of low, grey-green shrub willow. Sheep and cattle and deer in winter once grazed here freely and the willow got blitzed. Four years ago, this part of the moor was fenced off, the willow got its chance and in a few years' time the scrub will be trees.

19

Dave said I'd see crossbills at Coire Loch. Would I know one if I saw it? A small finch-like bird, it says in the book, 'with distinctive crossed mandibles' – i.e. a twisted beak. Good for cracking pine cones and getting to the seeds.

A narrow track winds through the pinewood, up and down and round about, till I reach the lochan – not so much a loch as a large pond, almost a perfect circle with boggy margins, surrounded by trees. It's just off the tourist drag in Glen Affric. A small burn filters into it on the far side. It's best seen from above, on a knoll with pine trees – where two young Japanese pose for a photograph by a craggy old pine.

I find the path below teeming with small frogs (toads?), olive green and slimy, some entwined in clumsy embrace, knots of them every two or three yards. It must be the mating season – not hopping but humping. They drag themselves along with hind legs outstretched. Croak, croak, croak. A sight to gladden naturalists but not me. Slimy things. Frog princes? No wonder the maiden hesitates to kiss.

I have to watch my step or I'll crush them underfoot. And not a crossbill in sight.

20

Old Duncan sits by a log fire glowing in the redbrick hearth. A weathered shepherd's stick is propped by the door. He hands me a sheaf of his reminiscences which he's had typed, hoping, I suspect, that I can help him get them published. In this I fail.

My eye lights on this: 'When I was only six – and there were two younger than me – an angel came and took our loving mother to the quiet gardens of another paradise.' How strange. Fey. It's not what I expected.

Duncan tells me he was born in 1914 and he worked as a shepherd, water gillie, stalker at the Chisholm Estate at Fasnakyle and, later, head stalker in Affric. He saw the dams go up in Affric and Glen Cannich and the great flood of December 1962 which swept away bridges in Affric and threatened to blow the dams.

The talk turns to wildlife and it seems that Old Duncan has a great contempt for conservationists, a feeling shared by many keepers, stalkers and farmers: 'They won't listen,' he says. Pine martens are a particular culprit when it comes to the decline of the capercaillie, the great bird of the pine forest, now a threatened species. He was keeping an eye on a caper nest with two eggs until the day he found the eggs smashed and pine marten droppings beside them. He says his hens were killed by a fox 'just for badness'. When vermin – his word – were kept down, other wildlife flourished. Keepers knew where the nests were and would leave some untroubled. In his view, keepers are the true conservationists.

Such is the wisdom, I find it hard to make a judgment. On the one hand, scientists produce their statistics; on the other, country folk like Duncan, who observe nature at first hand from one year to the next, assert the evidence of their own eyes. I sit on the fence.

21

I've seen the apocalypse. It's at the end of the road in Glen Cannich.

On this dreich day, mist hangs low over the hills and the rain is soft and insistent. The road out of Cannich village rises steeply, twisting and turning and at the high point of the pass a vista opens over the treetops, wave after wave of birch foliage seeming all the greener for the wet, like gentle oriental gardens gone to wilderness.

Then the road dips to follow the river, ultimately crossing by a bailey bridge. This is where, according to birdman Dave, an eagle may be seen. No big bird spirals upwards into the overcast. Some other day perhaps.

Here the enclosing trees pull back to open up a rugged countryside of high moorland and black craggy hills, the view ahead hemmed in by rocky slopes. Where exposed, the underlying bedrock glistens in the pale light. There are few dwellings. A wheelie bin stands at the end of a track, a long haul from the stalker's house a quarter of a mile away (on reflection, he probably drops it from his 4 x 4).

Lashing rain now – bracken and heather sodden at the roadside. Even so, there's a glamour about this quiet glen, so reclusive compared to Affric's blatant charms. The road rises inexorably until a last curve brings the dam into view, unseen until then, and the song dies on my lips.

A long black barrier extends half a mile across the whole width of the glen, hill to hill, a black concrete bastion only partially softened by wisps of mist. From this angle, there's no sign of the immense waters held behind it. Mullardoch's not just the longest dam in the land, it must be the ugliest – a monument to brutalism. The spirit of the place seems malign.

I scramble down to the marshy valley floor where a thin trickle of water emerges from the foot of the dam and runs into a pool on the first lap of its long journey eastwards to the North Sea. Once, when in spate, it would gush over cataracts. The dam wall, stained black with an algal growth, towers 160 feet above me, impounding a huge mass of water – the mere thought of it makes me quake. A walk across the top of the dam is quite as unsettling, with the sheer drop on one side and a grey choppy sea pent up on the other. A gleam of sunshine would soften the blow but there's no let-up in the weather.

A few souls live close by, even under the brow of the dam itself, where a lilliputian cottage sits on the riverbank. On the approach to the dam, a high white wall alongside the road masks a tall house mistakenly designated 'hotel' on the map. And, almost on the lip of the dam itself, a gate gives access to a timber house half hidden in trees. There's a pile of newly sawn logs beside the gate and a boat parked outside but Carl the Dane who lives there is not at home.

Below, another boat is beached just above the water line. There must be traffic on the loch.

Today I knock on the door and find Carl in. We sit in the modest kitchen – Carl and his wife Ninon and I, with jam jars and pickles and tins on the table and cups of tea in our hands. Bespectacled, wearing a rusty-coloured sweater, his close-cropped white hair ginger at the roots, Carl looks more like a farmer than Highland laird – and sonsie Ninon the picture of a farmer's wife.

Carl still has a home in Denmark, where he *was* a farmer and kept dairy cattle and pigs. But farmers get a raw deal, he says. 'Nobody likes farmers in Denmark and nobody likes them here.'

For much of the year, they live in this wooden house on the brink of Loch Mullardoch – I can't say overlooking the dam because trees hide the view. The garden at this autumnal season is spattered with fallen birch leaves.

The boat drawn up on the shore below is his. From May to September, he ferries parties of walkers and climbers halfway up the loch to reach the high hills.

When he was young, Carl worked for a year as a gamekeeper and thought he'd be a keeper for the rest of his life but his father put his foot down. 'No way to make a living,' he said and Carl stayed on grudgingly to end up running the home farm.

He came to Scotland to stalk deer in 1967 and wanted to buy a piece of land then but Ninon resisted. She must have had a change of heart because, 12 years later, he bought the Benula Estate in the mountainous country at the far end of the loch. As he grew older, he sold off much of it, though he still shoots over his own and other people's ground – sometimes visiting the deer forests south of Loch Ness.

Like so many others, Carl laments the perceived loss of wildlife in the Highlands. It's a recurring theme. The eagles have gone, he says. Twenty-five years ago, when he first came to live by the dam, he could count six pairs of golden eagles. This year, a man from the RSPB couldn't find any. Grouse, pheasant, white hares – there used to be lots of them but not any more. Black grouse – the same. In the past, he'd see maybe 40 black grouse at lek but hasn't seen a lek in the last couple of years. Ducks, too.

Once you could count 30 pairs of mallard. This year he's seen only one with ducklings and he'd seen none the year before.

He blames all licensed predators, with pine martens at the head of the list. Among their prey is the capercaillie, a threatened species. His neighbour had peacocks ('Screechy things,' he says with distaste) and a pine marten got them all. 'He got my geese, he got all my ducks except one.' But you can't shoot pine marten any more – it's illegal to kill them. In Carl's opinion, the best pine marten is a pine martin squashed flat on the road.

All hook-billed birds and red-toothed animals of the kind that used to be classed as vermin and harried mercilessly by farmers and gamekeepers are guilty in Carl's eyes. There are songbirds in the trees around his house. 'It's nice to see them on the bird table. Then the bloody sparrowhawk gets them.'

22

The Cannich river curves away from the road in a wide bend round a broad flat of heather and coarse grass. I call this spot the River Bend, with capitals. Here, the stream is broken by shallow cataracts and stony islets, each of them crowned by one or more hardy little trees. On the far side are tall pinewoods and a backdrop of dipping blue hills – Creag a Chorre Duibh, the Rock of the Black Corrie.

On a day when the river is in spate after heavy rain, I can hear it before I see it. Even in the car, the sound of turbulent waters is audible over the engine noise.

A stony tractor track leads towards the river and midway along, blocking the track, stands a parked caravan and car. A man at the open door of the caravan observes the rain glumly but, as I approach splashing through the puddles and prepared with a pleasantry, he retreats inside and slams the door behind him. Maybe he thinks I'm someone in authority who'll ask him to move on.

Above the broad river, I look down at the flood thrashing over rocky shelves and jutting boulders, splitting into many channels, surging in walls of solid water, tearing at islets in the stream, each surmounted with clusters of little trees. Whole hillsides brimming with water have fed this angry torrent. Just watching the maelstrom from my safe vantage point gives me a sudden frisson, something between fear and fascination.

A month later in London, standing in front of a painting by the Victorian artist John Everett Millais at an exhibition in Tate Britain, I experience a sense of déjà vu. The scene is in the Highlands and Millais called it *The Sound of Many Waters*. The artist set up his easel almost at river level looking upstream. Rocky islets part the floodwaters. Small trees sprout from the rocks. It might be the very scene at the River Bend. Only the woodland on the riverbanks – leaf trees in autumn colours in place of the dark pines – is the give-away. Millais took up his brush elsewhere. The nearest he's likely to have been to this glen was Loch Ness, where he painted ruined Urquhart Castle in a rainstorm. In fact, no artist of distinction seems to have found inspiration in Strathglass, which is surprising. And no poets either, now that I think of it. No Lakers here. I wonder why.

The sound of many waters echoes everywhere in this strath and these three glens. Trees, water and stone, the great trinity, the body and soul of Affric and Strathglass. Waters come in many forms: wide sheets of mirror glass reflecting sky and hill in calm weather or whipped into spindrift in a gale; little eyelet lochans bleared with underwater vegetation; freshets gurgling through the undergrowth unseen but loudly heard; mere squelches seeping through the moss; mad burns dashing over shelves of rock and eddying darkly at the base of falls. And always sensed beneath the green mantle or visible in naked extrusion, the presence of bedrock, age-old and everlasting foundation of all.

23

February. At the River Bend.

The water is still and untroubled now. There's a hush in the air. Thin bands of mist cling to the hillsides but the tops are clear in sunlight. There's snow on the higher hills and the far mountains are pure white. Upstream, where the river emerges from Loch Carrie, breaking ice sparkles in pale sunshine.

Catherine and I walk along the curve of the riverbank, following a faint grassy trail through stone-littered and rather boggy ground, with a multitude of small plant life at our feet – all kinds of delicate mossy fronds, lichens and fluted fungi among carpets of brown alder leaves. A pad of fungus raises little scarlet-tipped bell mouths to the air. A small stone the size of a melon is a botanic garden in miniature, capped with a profusion of little species – what botanists call the 'lower plants'. If Joe were here he'd name them all.

There's a brief intrusion. A yellow bin lorry comes speeding along where the road makes a cord with the river bend. So Monday must be bin day in the glen. Green wheelies wait at the farm lane ends. It'll take half the morning to collect the rubbish from the few households here – a country outing for the binmen and all in the day's work. How lucky for them.

24

Past Tomich a rough track in a field leads to a little gabled house with green scrollwork eaves, the oldest house in the district. Kyle, who manages the fishing on the Hill Lochs, lives there. If he's out on the loch today he'll get wet. The windscreen wipers are swishing.

Today I explore, being in search of a place out west called Cougie, which has passed into legend. The way some people talk you'd think it was the end of the world.

George at Upper Glassburn has directed me to take a 'scenic' route, which means tackling a steep muddy track through Plodda woods – Land Rover terrain, gouged and bouldered, which George no doubt takes at a lick on his postie run. George has many irons in the fire including delivering the post part-time and, for two days in the week, he drives a wee red van along the strath and up and down two glens with élan. But for me it's an obstacle course.

I emerge at last on the forestry road that leads to Cougie where the road surface is better but not much.

Sprays of muddy liquid squish from the wheels as I dodge the potholes. Some miles on, at a bend in the river at the forest edge, I reach an odd jumble of buildings – a low timber chalet, a cottage and a shed or two. I'm not impressed. This dreich weather does the place no favours – until I meet Val whose cheery greeting brightens the day.

Val is the chatelaine at Cougie, a large lady with frisking hair who talks with a hint of Welsh in her accent. She invites me to sit with her on the veranda with the rain dripping on the plastic canopy over our heads. Hens pick about in the ground in front of us – these unconcerned birds are survivors. 'A pine marten got six of them the other night,' she says.

Birds flit by. 'Goldcrests,' she says. 'We get a lot of bullfinches some years. Some years they strip the cherry tree and there's no blossom next spring.'

Val runs part of the long chalet as a hostel for walkers. Trekkers walking between the west coast and Affric often arrive on her doorstep. A name board on a door with the letters scored into the wood means nothing to me. Gaelic? In fact it's Arabic, inscribed there when her daughter lived with a Moroccan partner. The inscription seems less exotic and romantic when you know that it translates as wooden hut.

Returning, I take the back road from Cannich to Struy alongside the River Glass. Fishermen stand like statues thigh-high in its dark waters. A herd of Sheena's cattle, black and red, are grazing on its low-lying meadows.

Sheena is the daughter of Iain Thomson, a man of many talents who has turned his hand to writing. He's been a cattle farmer and, before that, he was a shepherd at Strathmore at the head of Loch Monar in the far reaches of Glen Strathfarrar. He wrote a fine book about his experiences there and, since then, has published others. I pass the old caravan parked by farm buildings where he writes. It's a tubby little vehicle, elderly, a bit the worse for wear and looks as if it could accommodate two at a squeeze. He's writing a novel now.

Near Struy, I stop at a two-storey timber house where, leaning on the five-bar gate at the top of the drive, I chat with Tim. Tim's an ecologist and woodland consultant. I first met him when he was warden at Beinn Eighe Nature Reserve in the north-west Highlands. He says he loved the job but got fed up with the increasing bureaucracy. He was lucky to find this place – he bought 13 acres across the river from Struy, built the house and now he has his own young cattle to fulfil a long-held ambition. Somewhat incongruously for a man of green credentials, he's a sports car enthusiast. When he was young, he and his brother used to race souped-up Austin 7s. He's moved on since then. Parked at the side of the house are a 4x4, a mud-spattered Jag and a vintage Porsche under wraps.

25

George's home at Upper Glassburn is a rambling two-storey house with gabled windows in the roof and a porch framed by rustic columns made from pine trunks. The house stands high above a sharp bend in the road between Cannich and Struy overshadowed by trees. Turning into the lane calls for caution since traffic (what there is of it) tends take the corner at speed. There's a bed-and-breakfast sign attached to a tree at the lane end.

At the top of the stairs in this house hangs a small painting, naive in style, of a green-hulled fishing boat (I called it a smack – which George took as a slight) buffeting through white-crested waves. 'The *Janet*,' says George, 'my first boat.' George skippered her as a young man fishing off the west coast.

When he came ashore for good, he thought there was money to be made cutting peat – no shortage of peat in the Highlands – and imported a peat harvester from Finland. Unfortunately the enterprise failed. But George is not easily defeated and, when a friend stopped him in the street and asked if he could drive a lorry, he jumped at the chance. Next morning at the crack of dawn, he was at the wheel of a clapped-out truck blasting out exhaust fumes, clanking up the Oban brae with a load of granite kerbstones bound for the outer isles. The business prospered.

George declined the offer of a partnership in favour of a percentage of the turnover, a deal which gave him the funds to buy the Cnoc Hotel at Struy plus the inn across the road, where he made a genial host and his wife Ishbel cooked good, plain meals for the guests.

The hotel, a row of converted cottages on a grassy bank just out of Struy, has a cheery look when the lights are lit and the inn has come up in the world since its days as a country howff with an earthen floor. The joke was that, in winter, you had to drink up fast before the beer froze in the glass.

George also sings. There's a pile of CDs for sale on the sideboard at Upper Glassburn featuring him and his son John in an hour's worth of folk song – 'Ca' the Yowes' and 'Scots Wha' Hae' and such – which they recorded at the old ferryman's cottage down the strath at Aigas.

George has sung his songs to guests at Aigas, the baronial tower house on the road to Beauly where the naturalist Sir John Lister-Kaye lives and from where he runs an upmarket field centre. Courses there include heritage tours, which I guess have a special appeal to American visitors. I can imagine George on a festive night charming the Americans with song and story – bearded as he is, dressed for the occasion in the kilt, the very image of a minstrel Scot.

26

This morning, there's honey for breakfast at Upper Glassburn, special honey, delicious, the colour of old bronze and crusty at the rim of the jar. 'There's a story about that,' says George. For sure, there's always a story with George. He knows everyone and their stories too.

For example, the formidable lady from America, 'slightly hippy but not short of cash', who bought the old stables near Guisachan House where she planned to live the green life. The first frosts of winter put paid to that dream and she promptly returned to the States though she continued to visit every summer. She'd shipped in a consignment of essential provisions in bulk (George says by the ton), including a load of

Mexican honey. George helped her out now and again doing odd jobs like mowing the lawn. When she finally sold the stables, she asked if he'd like a sum of money. '*A sum of money*?' George was taken aback but rallied, made a joke of it and named a tentative figure.

It has to be said here that George's hearing isn't perfect.

'A *tub* of *honey*,' she repeated crisply.

George left with a barrel of honey in the back of his truck and guests at Upper Glassburn sample it yet. He says there's two or three hundredweight still in his garage. It must be 40 years old by now and still maturing and no doubt all the better for that.

Personalities spring to life in George's conversation – Janet the Wheel in Tomich whose simple paintings were 'discovered' by an American academic who hailed her as a primitive of genius. Alas, her fame didn't last. Why the Wheel? Even George who knows everything doesn't know that, only that she came from a long line of Wheels.

And there were the genteel females, not young, who booked into Upper Glassburn while attending an alternative lifestyle retreat nearby called the Centre of Light. 'I called them Linda's Lassies,' says George. 'They tended to be women of a certain age. I suppose they spent their time chanting and banging drums and communing with the spiritual.' One guest would eat nothing cooked – to Ishbel's dismay, all her meals were 'raw fruitarian' (not my phrase – I read it in a newspaper). Heaped bean sprouts were a staple. But then Linda moved her Centre of Light elsewhere with accommodation provided and now bean sprouts are off the menu at Upper Glassburn.

In the long evenings at George and Ishbel's, George, whisky in hand, can be persuaded to reminisce. From his time at the Cnoc Hotel, there's his tale of the English barrister, very pukka, clipped of speech, stiff-backed as befits a former officer in the Guards. But it was the wife who wore the trousers. She managed everything, even laying out his clothes in the morning, though not always to his satisfaction. 'George,' he said at breakfast parade, as he called it (always at eight hundred hours precisely), 'George,' he said, 'I found 16 points of error in my kit today.' Then, sotto voce: 'Say nothing – wife watching.'

One night when all the guests had retired to bed, perhaps after a nightcap or two, strange sounds were heard overhead. Thump, thump, thump, then silence. Thump, thump, thump again. And so on. George and Ishbel were somewhat alarmed. George decided to investigate and as he reached the top of the stairs he was confronted by the barrister marching down the corridor, stark naked. He snapped smartly to attention, looked George straight in the eye and without a word strode on. At this point, a bedroom door opened and a woman's arm reached out, grabbed the naked barrister by the neck and pulled him inside.

Next morning, he appeared immaculately turned out as usual, not at the stipulated eight hundred hours but five minutes early. 'Appalling behaviour, George,' he said stiffly. 'Are you going to throw me out?' George assured him he wouldn't but was unable to confirm that no one else had seen the episode. All through breakfast, as the guests entered and were hailed by George – 'And did you sleep well?' – the barrister suffered agonies of embarrassment while his wife sat stony-faced.

Once, Tom Sharpe, the satirical novelist (*Porterhouse Blue* and the Wilt novels), and his wife called at Upper Strathglass for afternoon tea and decided to stay the night. At dinner, George observed him moving from table to table between courses, seating himself with different guests in turn. George was puzzled and quizzed him about it later.

Research, answered Sharpe. Talking to strangers gave him ideas for his books – a story here, a catchphrase there, an anecdote, a line of dialogue, a quirky detail, a character study. Thus Mrs Sharpe had learned to eat alone.

George, I imagine, didn't mention the naked barrister.

27

Upper Glassburn, evening. I arrive to find George and Ishbel sitting with two hillwalking guests, David and Alastair, a glass in their hands. I get a dram too. David is burly, stoutish, a retired schoolmaster from Oxford. Alastair's lean, an actuary in Edinburgh – possibly he attacks hills as a relief from his desk job. He's a Munroist, now polishing off the peaks around Affric, Glen Cannich and Strathfarrar – two today. David follows behind. He says he aims from one boulder ahead to the next, so his hill climbing is calibrated by the higher stones. Today he sat on a rock in the sunshine while Alastair pushed to the top.

Alistair spreads out a map showing all the hills he's climbed circled in pencil, one tight group interlocking like the Olympic logo. Sgurr na Lapaich is marked off, Tom a' Choinich, Mam Sodhail, Carn Eighe and several more. Tomorrow he'll round off with Carn nan Gobhar above Loch Mullardoch, which sparks my interest. I might join him.

David tells me that, before he retired, he was headmaster of the King Edward School in Oxford, rather a prestigious place, I imagine. Yet his origins were humble. He spent his boyhood in Bo'ness on the Firth of Forth where, at the age of seven, he learned that he was adopted. At 19 he was taken on as an unqualified teacher at a tough village school near Stirling. When he asked how to keep order, he was told, 'Belt the hell out of them.' Once he was mystified when a boy knocked on the classroom door and asked if he'd any shoes. 'Only what I'm wearing,' he answered and the boy retreated without a word. Later he learned the school ran a cobbling class and shoes for repair were collected every week. It sounds like good practical education – not on offer now, I guess.

He progressed – went to college and ended up lecturing. After a spell at an international school in Luxembourg, he was headhunted by Winchester before moving to Oxford. And he still speaks with a good Scots accent.

David, stiff from his climbing, heads for home, leaving Alastair to his final hill. As we drive up Glen Cannich, I fight to keep pace with the lemon yellow coupé as Alastair flings it round the bends and twists of the road. He's a man in a hurry.

We park under the bleak wall of the dam, where stags with ragged coats are browsing. We search but do not find a reasonable track at the end of the loch. By rights there ought to be a route along the shore but the grey bouldery waterline, scored by fluctuating water levels, offers no practical access. Down below us on the grey foreshore – you can't truly describe it as a beach – we see Carl the Dane's boat hauled up with a tractor beside it but there's no sign of a track along that rocky shoreline. Alastair says they paid Carl a tenner each a couple of days ago to reach the hills at the far end of the loch and back.

Mud, mud, black peat and stony ruts gouged by some vehicle. Spongy and waterlogged, it's hard walking till we find traces of a barely defined track. We contour above the loch, avoiding the worst bogs, till we reach the Mullardoch burn which we follow upwards. This echoing burn enlivens a dark landscape of muted browns, greens and greys turning to black as it tumbles over shelves of rock, pausing briefly in shallow pools where (a passing thought) it would be good to plunge into on a summer's day. It is not that day. The reach of loch below us is the colour of slate. Spits of rain turn to a steady drizzle. Strands of mist cling to the tops and a band of cloud looming on the horizon indicates bad weather on the way.

We are lapped by rounded hills crumbling here and there into rocky outcrops, with a band of snow under what could be (but isn't, of course) the summit ridge. Carn nan Gobhar (Hill of the Goats) is no craggy fell but a featureless dumpling 'of no great distinction' in the words of the Munro book. Nevertheless, for the true Munroist (not me), it must be scaled. Alastair, tall, fit and trim, strides upwards and I grit my teeth and keep pace step for step with an increasingly leaden distaste.

Why am I doing this?

Somewhere above the 600-metre mark my determination falters. I'm conscious that nothing will be seen from the top in this weather. I'm tired, not at my best, and my spirit fails.

Go ahead, Alastair, I'll loiter here.

I watch him advance to the head of the glen, a lone figure moving fast and briefly silhouetted against the sky. I'd expected to see him turn to the left and continue to what appears to be the summit ridge but he disappears from sight. This is another hilltop that hides itself behind a bulky shoulder.

Now that I've abdicated from the climb, I can wander over to the burn with a clear conscience and watch how it tumbles from one still pool to the next, finding more to attract me in its secret hollows than in the broad brushstrokes of the glowering hills. Ambling downwards beside the burn, I stop to inspect the solitary tree we passed on the ascent when we were pushing on with no time to glance aside. Trees always attract me – I wrote a book about them once. Twin trunks rise from the root then split to form four slender stems. Smooth pale bark and an early flush of leaves opening penny-bright tell me it's an aspen – not exactly a rarity in these parts but not as common as other species native to the Highlands – birch, pine and alder, to name three. Aspen is the shaking tree, the trembling one, *Populus tremula* to give it its official name, because of the way its foliage shivers and shimmers in a breeze.

I love aspens. I like their disc leaves peppered on thread-like stalks, uncurling in spring, as now, like little flames on bare branches, and, in the autumn, making a golden glory. This tree is reclusive, a lone specimen in a seemingly treeless desert, hidden for half its height in a gully, rooted at the water's edge where the burn runs over lichen-spotted rock. The bank is steep, almost vertical, and I view it from above.

'Aspen seldom forms a tall tree; it is most often seen as a thicket of sucker shoots in some marshy spot.' I quote the forest writer Herbert Edlin, one who knows. Seldom tall? In this case, well, tallish. On the elevated bank high above its roots I now discover a host of suckers unnoticed before. At my boot, on the narrow track itself, springs one little twig carrying a single infant leaf tinged dark green shading to bronze and red and then I find another and another and yet more. They spread over a surprisingly wide radius, little torches on spindly stems, bristling through the vegetation, none more than a foot high. The root system must extend cup-like from the gully bottom to the top of the bank. A small shoot, bearing twin-fretted leaves, pokes up defiantly from a knobble of root exposed on the narrow track and polished by many passing feet. Elsewhere, it might hope to make a tree. But this dwarf growth expends its energy in vain. Each shoot shows the telltale signs of having been bitten off by deer. They'll never flourish.

At length a diminutive figure crests the skyline – Alastair returning. He says the last section to the summit was a little steep and there was a flurry of snow as he stopped to eat a sandwich at the top. At my level, there was only rain. One more Munro has fallen to him – only nine more to go. By summer, he expects to tick off his last peak. There'll be a small celebration at the top for a few family and friends, hopefully on a more elegant hill than this. Back at the dam wall, we part and ahead of me the yellow coupé streaks down the glen in serpentine flight.

28

Caravan park, Sunday morning, 8 a.m. Catherine is here for the weekend in search of dragon- and damselflies – her latest thing. Glen Affric is a hotspot on the dragonfly map.

Across the road at Marydale, Sister Petra Clare rings the bell – we're up late. Crispy bacon rolls for breakfast, an indulgence. Hail cholesterol.

So, a leisurely start. At the Coire Loch, we splodge around in the mossy, reedy margins and find a black darter and then a common hawker which C tries to photograph but it's too quick for her – a tantalising gleam of blue on diaphanous wings, never settling. Here, there, gone.

We progress up the glen, still on the lookout. Small Loch Salach a' Ghiubhais would be promising, she says, if only the sun would shine, which it doesn't. Still, there's a common hawker to record and one butterfly, a meadow brown. Not a lot, but she's satisfied.

29

There's snow on the hills and menacing clouds. 'It's a thin wind still,' says Donny, who looks after the Guisachan cottages for Donald Fraser. Thin, meaning sharp, keen, biting.

The bare birch woods are red against the hillsides.

In Tomich, asking directions at the inn, I see a sprightly, elderly man walking his dog down the road. 'Albert Dormer,' says my informant.

'He used to be bridge correspondent for *The Times*.' When he lived in Tomich? 'No, that was before.'

What chance brought him here to live?

30

Catherine and I walk down the road at Guisachan in the dark, with a faint moon glimpsed through the foliage. The clock tower at the steading is ghostly in the mirk, like the gothic house in *Psycho*. It's pitch black under the trees but we have torches and, at the foot of the drive, there are lights, a line of globes glowing faintly. Moths have landed on some of the globes. C identifies a winter moth and a few pale brindled beauties.

31

One of the Tomich cottages is for sale and, on a whim, we call to view. We fall in love. It's perfect – it's the home in Affric we've always wanted. For three days and nights, we dream.

But we're not country folk. It's not for us.

32

Albert Dormer, who's in his 80s, came to live in Tomich 15 years ago when he tired of London. He found the cottage by chance on a house-hunting trip north with his ex-wife, who encouraged him to buy. He says she probably thought it was fine to live 500 miles apart. It could have been further. They'd looked at a house on the Pentland Firth.

His dog Pickles, a bouncy ginger poodle, jumps on my lap when I sit down on the settee, followed by a Siamese cat who curls herself alongside. Like commas. Both accept stroking.

For years, Albert, a tournament player, was bridge correspondent for *The Times* and he's written several books on the game. Through bridge, he met Jaime Ortiz-Patino, wealthy grandson of a tin-mining magnate in

Bolivia, bridge player and owner of the Valderrama golf course in Spain, and together they travelled on behalf of the World Bridge Federation. Patino had a mission to stamp out cheating in the international game. (Albert says the Italians were the worst.)

He no longer plays. Instead he takes Pickles for long walks in the morning, reads the newspapers, watches a little television and feeds the geese in his garden.

33

The weather's turned cold again, with snow on the tops. Rain drummed on the caravan roof overnight and, outdoors, the wind nips. There's been one downpour already and, in spite of a few ragged blue patches in the sky, there will be more. Dark clouds moving fast on the horizon give promise of squalls to come.

Not the best day to explore the loch country on high moorland between Affric and Glen Moriston. Nevertheless . . .

Hilton pond beyond Tomich is a circle of ornamental water in front of a big white house where there's said to be an osprey's nest in the trees. I can't find it. How can you tell? What does an osprey nest look like?

A track leads into mixed woodland – conifers, birch and rowan and, here and there, an old pine, all tangled with grey-green lichens. The mossy ground squelches with water. It's all a dripping dampness. But the track has a stony surface, laid down possibly for pony traffic between the glens, and boots ring out pleasantly on it.

A burn almost worthy of being called a river flows fast alongside, gushing over the track where the map shows a ford – it's no great obstacle, I can splash through with feet more or less dry. Then I come on a notice – 'Wild boar reservation 200 metres ahead' – and, beyond it, the high perimeter fence of an enclosure. I'm glad of this fence. How wild are wild boars, after all? They have tusks.

But, when a couple of dun-coloured beasts emerge from the woods and trot along on their side of the barrier, they seem innocuous – smaller than I expected and peaceable. A second billboard informs that the reservation has been set up with various scientific objectives in view, including studies into the effect of boars on vegetation, such as tree regeneration, and the prospects of farming them. Boar steaks.

I walk on with one more river to cross – a burn, rather. A hop and a leap onto the grassy bank on the other side bring me to a stile at the woodland edge, with open moorland beyond. Wreckage of a footbridge a little off the track indicates what must have been another route, now abandoned. Here the burn is spanned by two parallel tree trunks, or possibly old telegraph poles, with a few rotten planks nailed across and a gap where the remainder are missing. A single small pine and a leafless, warped birch tree stand guard.

Ahead is an intrusion – a pylon. Tall, unfriendly, gaunt against the lowering sky. And not alone but one of a chain carrying the electricity transmission line from Beauly southward to connect with the grid. I see the wires looping from pylon to pylon in diminishing perspective down towards Tomich and beyond. Ugly enough as they are, there is worse to come – the electricity company plans to replace them with giants up to twice their height to carry power from the new wind farms mushrooming in the north. This is not a prospect I like and nor do many of the locals. There's going to be an inquiry.

It's cold. The path deteriorates as it ascends steeply towards the pass, cut into channels by winter weather and the lack of maintenance. Rivulets run down it.

The wind freshens. Murky clouds rear on the horizon and a veil of precipitation drifts over the hills as dirty weather sweeps in. Soon all to the west is blotted out. Light fades and the first flecks of snow float on the wind, thickening by the minute until it's a perfect welter. The hoped-for view down from the top of the pass seems ever less certain and it takes little self-persuasion to turn back for home.

The sheltered wood is an altogether friendlier place than the open moor. Softly falling snowflakes drift through the trees. A lattice bridge (unmarked on the map) is a good place to pause, to watch the agitated waters of the burn below and warm cold fingers round a cup of hot soup from the flask.

34

Liz lives in a grass-roofed ecological house in the hamlet of Knockfin. She's a scientist, a botanist, and the boars were her idea. She calls them her 'piggies'.

There are canoes under a canopy at the door and a stack of wood at the side of the house. Behind the house, the hillside rises steeply to a line of birches, with the ground in between covered in grass and heather and swathes of bracken.

Liz says nobody likes bracken. It spreads like wildfire, kills all other plants and it's practically indestructible. But she reckoned her piggies would do the trick. They root out and eat the tough rhizomes in the soil and they feed on the young shoots when they first poke through and fronds begin to unfurl –just the thing for the hillside behind the house, where she could study their impact on the vegetation.

Not everyone was as enthusiastic as she. Folk envisioned wild boar running loose and attacking them on their country walks. The community council split over the question and it was only when the Forestry Commission offered a piece of woodland near Hilton and funding to go with it that the project could go ahead.

Most of the animal management and care is done by Rae, a local forester, but Liz takes her turn at feeding time. She admits it can be a little scary. When the sows sense her presence they scurry from the wood, snuffing and puffing around her, to be followed by Boris the boar ambling down at a more stately pace. He's harmless enough, she says, but he's big and she's small and slim and she feels uneasy in his presence.

'Come and see them,' she says. 'Come at feeding time.'

35

Rae loves his pigs. You can see it in his face. Catherine and I join him on a visit to the piggies. There's a thin covering of snow as we drive into the woods over a bumping track

Rae swings open the metal gate and leads us into the enclosure. No sign of animal life as yet. All's quiet in the forest – until he tips a bag of feed into the wooden trough and, on his call, a file of chunky long-snouted beasts, sows and their piglets, dark in the coat, some tinged with auburn, materialise from the trees and cluster round the trough.

Boris delays his appearance. He's last on the scene, an actor making his entrance and not intending to be upstaged. Or perhaps he was just deeper in the trees than his familiars. Down the hill he saunters at last, picking his way among a brash of broken branches. Once at the trough, he shoulders his way through for his breakfast.

We admire his rough coat, his furry heart-shaped ears and the short curled pile on his flanks. At first, I don't see his tusks, which I'd imagined as long scimitars, but not so. They're small, tucked neatly in his jaws but interlocking and businesslike nevertheless. Rae says the grinding together of upper and lower fangs keeps them sharp. I can imagine my shinbone crunched between them.

But Rae, giving Boris a gentle pat on the back, says he's not dangerous – though he adds a caveat: 'Don't take him by surprise.' And further: 'You won't outrun a boar.' They have to get used to you. 'Keep talking to them, talk all the time and they'll accept you.'

Rae says pigs have their own words, special sounds which mean different things that allow them to communicate. He hears them conversing at night – they're naturally nocturnal animals and this daytime feeding is not their normal habit. Acorns and beech nuts are their preferred diet – thin pickings around here, where oak and beech trees are uncommon – but they'll root out the fleshy bracken tubers. Which, of course, is why they're here.

A fence divides their enclosure from the adjacent woodland and the difference in ground vegetation is marked. Deep heather and bracken flourishes on the pig-free ground but, on our side of the fence, it's been hoovered. And there's new growth, too. Rae shows us the proof – a sprinkling of inch-high feathery green shoots poking through the snow. These are infant pines, showing that the trees can regenerate here once the ground vegetation is disturbed. All the area where we stand was pinewood until the foresters cut down the best trees for timber, sparing only few gnarled specimens – the picturesque spreading pine trees we like to see now. Then they planted commercial conifers of foreign origin, quick to grow, soon to harvest. Green shoots at our feet show that the native forest can return.

Meanwhile, Boris and friends gobble greedily, their soft snuffling muzzles deep in the trough. Cuddly though they look, they're not pets. These little piggies are heading for market: 'Monday is pig day at Dingwall,' says Rae. But don't mention the word abattoir. Rae won't have it. He may be pragmatic about their fate but he prefers the dignity of plain English for their end. 'I don't like the word. I say slaughterhouse.'

Agreed. Who'd want to read a book called *Abattoir-Five*?

36

It's a wild morning, with lowering sky, wind-driven clouds and pelting rain filling potholes up to the brim on the Plodda road.

Off the road and into the wood there's barely a sound or stir, only a pattering on the leaves overhead. A lane leads downhill through tall grey trunks but everything else is green – the grass, the moss mantling the earth and the rocks and stumps of trees felled long ago. I suspect that the lane, now muddy and rutted, with jutting boulders, may once have been a carriage drive leading to the ruined house of Guisachan. It's a bumpy ride.

We find Dave the tree-feller, a stocky greybeard, sizing up the standing timber, all these columns in a shady temple, glancing about, touching a stem here and there, looking up into the green canopy, gauging by eye alone the girth and height of Douglas firs planted more than a century ago.

The Douglas fir is a splendid tree. In maturity, its trunk is tall and ramrod straight, the rough bark gouged by russet fissures. When felled, the heartwood shows a delicious cream and red in cross-section. Boat-builders love it.

Dave selects his tree after careful scrutiny. 'Saw's blunt,' he says, seating himself on a stump with the chainsaw across his knees, sharpening the teeth with a small file. Dave, a freelance forester, says he has been cutting timber all his life, mainly in the south of England where he learned the trade from his father in the era of the horse, the axe and crosscut saw. For preference, he says, he likes to fell old hardwood trees like oak or beech. His busiest time ever was after the great gale of '87 which tumbled the woodland trees wholesale.

His strategy is to guide a falling tree between two neighbours so that their side branches will slow its descent and prevent it snapping when it hits the ground. Suppose it swings out of true? He gives me a wry look, shakes his head: 'It won't.'

He bends to the tree and the saw roars, spitting an arc of sawdust as the chain bites into the wood. With two swift applications, he cuts out a crescent of timber (he calls it a 'dob') then moves round the trunk to cut towards the newly made notch. As the saw slices deeper, his young assistant Neil hammers in a metal wedge behind it to prevent the chain jamming.

Can this be dangerous? I edge towards a nearby forest giant, aiming to dodge behind it in case of need.

I should have known better. There's a loud crack. (No one shouts 'Timber!') The tree teeters, tilts, tiptoes almost, then falls downwards with gathering speed, tearing through a mass of foliage to hit the ground with a thump. A slow shiver runs along the stem, snakelike, as if life is easing out of it as it comes to rest on the designated spot. Cut down in its prime – though a centenarian, it's a stripling in terms of its natural span.

Taking up the saw again, Dave shears off the side branches and measures the length – more than 160 feet from butt to tip – from which he cuts a usable length of 70 feet. A big tree but not the biggest he has cut down in Plodda. 'A fine stick,' says he. All trees great or small are sticks to the forester.

The Douglas firs extracted from Plodda are high-grade timber, much more valuable than the spruce trees harvested in their thousands. Can the wood survive the loss of so many fine specimens? It seems so. The fellers argue that since thinning creates life-giving light and space the forest will be enhanced rather than injured by the loss of a select few stems.

Not everyone agrees. Dave says he was harangued last week by a woman, an American volunteer for Trees for Life who have a base nearby. She accused him of vandalism, of dealing mortal blows to the living wood. Every tree was sacred in her eyes. He gave the stock answer – he was creating space for new growth. A tree falls – as it must in nature, given time – light floods in, seeds germinate, new trees grow. He doesn't think she was convinced.

Now the skidder lurches forward. The skidder is a huge tractor on fat wheels, each one taller than a man and laced with a web of chains to grip in the soft ground. Sitting high in the cab, Dave manoeuvres it into position then climbs down to help Neil sling a chain round the butt end of the tree and another felled earlier. He remounts and the machine moves off dragging the twin logs behind.

The ground in Plodda wood is treacherous, wildly uneven, boggy in parts and thick with trees – a challenge to the driver dragging six tons of lively timber behind him. The skidder rears and plunges, the logs buck and ply, gouging the soil and ripping through the undergrowth, smashing small timber en route to the roadside pick-up point. Down it plunges into the green chasm of a ravine, churning soil into a brown sludge where a small burn flows, barely visible in its mossy carpet at the best of times and now a quagmire. An elephant extracting teak from the jungle might be daintier but there are no elephants in Affric.

37

Walking through Plodda woods, Catherine and I find timber stacks where trees have been newly harvested. The ground's badly churned, and tree debris lies all around. Among the litter are wedges cut from the base of the trees by the chainsaw – crescents of freshly cut timber beautifully patterned, with a bright orange core. Dobs, as Dave the woodman called them.

We stagger back to the car with a couple in our arms – they're a fair weight – with the idea of varnishing them to preserve the colour. They'll look handsome and ornamental somewhere. (But in the end we don't.)

On our way back to Comar Lodge, we stop at the cemetery at Fasnakyle. A tall, thin elderly man, slightly stooped, is brushing leaves from a grave under the trees. We think he's a gardener at first but it's Old Duncan tidying his wife's grave. He doffs his cap to Catherine and she's charmed by the courtesy.

38

Back to Cougie, where the Pococks live in cheerful isolation. Cougie, way out west, is seven miles or more from Tomich and several from the nearest habitation. It's an isolated clearing in the woods – a few flat fields with a river running through and a huddle of low buildings, mainly timber, reached by a hard-packed forestry road badly in need of repair after winter damage. It's an oasis of open ground in the midst of dark forest.

A white-painted stone cottage, the only one of its kind, used to be the keeper's house for the neighbouring landowner, the Dutchman, Kwint. Mr Kwint had bad luck after the keeper left – later tenants did a moonlight flit and then squatters trashed the place – and he decided to sell. In the sales pitch, it sounded idyllic, but though potential buyers came in numbers they didn't buy. In the end, the Pococks made an offer and it was theirs.

The Pococks, father, mother and a vanload of family, had arrived one day out of the blue and stayed on as tenants and then owner-occupiers. There they sat tight, resisting all subsequent offers to buy them out from interested parties including the Forestry Commission whose trees surround them like a green ocean.

What brought them from the Welsh valleys to settle in this outpost? Val's husband John, stocky, grey-haired, sunk deep in a battered sofa in the living room, tells the story, with the occasional comment from wife in the kitchen, where she has venison sizzling in the pan.

They'd fallen in love with Scotland. Every year the family would head north in a Bedford work bus converted to seat a growing squad of children, chugging along narrow Highland roads in a cloud of exhaust fumes on the lookout for a site for their two bell tents. Camping holidays were fine but John, fretting at his office desk in the Welsh coalfields, wanted more. An offer of promotion felt like the first nail in his coffin and he decided to quit before the lid closed. A wild goose chase in the Bedford took father, mother and children rattling over to the remote Applecross peninsula in the north-west where he'd heard there were crofts for sale. They arrived to find . . . no crofts for sale in Applecross.

On the off chance, John walked into the Forestry Commission office in Inverness. In those days, it was the commission's policy to take on men to work part-time as foresters, with the enticement of a smallholding to supplement their wages off-season – a few acres and a cow or a pig for pioneering families.

John enquired.

'Nothing doing,' said the man behind the desk. On second thoughts: 'There's a place called Cougie but you wouldn't be interested in that.'

'Tell me about it,' says John.

'You wouldn't want it.'

'Try me,' says John.

The forestry man listed all the drawbacks. It was isolated, there was no water, it was damp . . .

'Fine,' says John.

Reluctantly, he was handed the keys and off they set cross-country again, past Tomich and heading into the unknown. Val pipes up from the kitchen: 'Halfway along the road, before we'd even seen the place, I said this is it. This feels like home.'

They got to the wooden house in Cougie to find it in darkness with the windows boarded up and the previous occupants' belongings still scattered about. But it still felt good.

'We took it on the spot,' says John.

After a spell as a forestry trapper armed with shotgun and rifle, shooting animals harmful to growing trees like rabbits and deer, he joined a Forestry Commission tree-planting squad. There's a line of trees on the skyline above the house, the fringe of a great plantation. 'I planted those,' says John. 'I planted a million trees with *this* –' and he takes up an old spade propped against the wall, the blade worn wafer thin with use.

Now John's trees have reached harvesting size and will soon be cut down. He dug them in on the bare moorland 40 years ago and soon he'll see them felled.

39

Mr Kwint, whose land abuts the Pococks' domain, is a little hard to locate. He's fishing, he's shooting or just not around. His home is in the Netherlands and he visits only half a dozen times in the year, living in the old manse at Fasnakyle, a house seen through the trees near the power station.

Really he'd like to be closer to his land at West Guisachan but his attempts to have a more convenient house built have failed to win planning approval. The bureaucrats, so it's said, consider it might disturb nesting ospreys. A victory for the local wildfowl? Or is there more to it than that? I suspect undercurrents.

Mr Kwint invites me in, stooping in the door frame (he's a lanky lad), and then sprawls at ease in armchair. There are books on the shelf and drinks on the table beside him.

His English is impeccable. It seems that his parents were enamoured of all things English and even spoke English in the home. By the age of seven he was fluent.

England is embedded in his name, Renynout Anthony Kornelious Gideon – Anthony after Anthony Eden, Churchill's foreign secretary and later prime minister, whom his mother admired. Like Eden, her boy turned out to be tall, slim and debonair.

There was music in the family home and he plays the violin and goes to concerts, which distinguishes him from most lairds in the Scottish

Highlands, native or foreign. But he enjoys the traditional lairdly pursuits. His love of fishing began at the age of five when he met boys fishing in the canal and asked for a shot at their rod – which was simply a bamboo cane. He says he was fascinated by the sight of the float bobbing on the water. Next day, he was back at the canal with basic tackle acquired from the local shop and that was the start of a long devotion.

Shooting came later – mostly roe deer in Denmark, followed by several years stalking red deer on trips to various Scottish estates until West Guisachan came on the market in 1994. Now friends and relatives fill the house at Fasnakyle in the stalking season.

There's a photograph on the wall of an Argocat – the stalker's vehicle – capsized on the moor. The accident happened when he tried to reverse on a steep bank and he and his brother were toppled into the peat. 'We landed face to face, never having been so intimate in 60 years.'

40

Next time in Cougie, I find the forest road much improved. That's to say the potholes are mostly filled in – it's still a rough ride. Every winter, the timber trucks tear it up and in spring it gets patched.

Cougie in sunshine is transformed. John, Val and I sit on the veranda under a fluttering Union Jack. It feels colonial. A stretch of green field lies before us with a cow or two at the far end and a couple of piglets romping. The pigs have reddish coats and curiously long snouts; they look a bit boarish. Of course they do. They're a cross between wild pig and a Tamworth, which is where the red comes from. The sow lies at her ease, a fat lady sunning herself. Through this bucolic scene, the river winds between heaped boulder banks where there are signs of engineering work – the family's handiwork, no doubt. (They're used to hard labour. Val says they had to dig six miles of trench for a cable in order to get online.) A blue boat swings midstream on its painter. It feels like Arcadia.

Returning on the forest road I stop by the Riabhach Burn and get out of the car. Down the slope, below my feet, there's a brown and peaty pool where the current cuts into the bank. I scramble down the grassy bank to the water's edge for a closer look at three alder trees on the far side, wizened and grey with lichen. (I watch trees a lot.) The burn's maybe three yards wide at this point.

There's a sudden movement at the water's edge. An otter, grey-sleek, swims out from the bank, busily nosing here and there, hump back glistening. Suddenly he (Is it a he? I wouldn't know) torpedoes through the water, twisting and turning, then stops and lifts his whiskery head, a fish held in its jaws. He catches sight of me and we eye each other, both motionless, for long seconds. Then he's off, bounding through the shallows and over the humpy grass, loping and sinuous, towards the forest.

It's the first time I've seen an otter in the wild. On a wet day as the rain plasters my hair and drips off my nose. Such sightings are a benison. A joy.

41

The door swings open – bang! – and three jolly fishermen burst into the bar at the Tomich inn, laughing and joking: 'Three degrees and *snowing* – it's chilly up there!' Much rubbing of hands. And: 'Osprey didn't stay long, did he? Five minutes and he was off.'

And this is May!

Two are dressed in plus-twos (breeches), fishing jackets and green socks. The third wears an olive green sweater with elbow patches and a hole in the back, deerstalker hat with a hedgehog of flies hooked around it, a red-and-white spotted kerchief round his neck and trousers with a big damp patch at the seat which steams gently when he takes his stance at the fire with his backside to the flames. He'll be the gillie.

'The best gillie in Scotland,' the burly one (an Englishman) shouts across to the landlord, tall, slim and bearded (another Englishman), and the gillie smiles modestly. Possibly he thinks so too. As fishermen do, they discuss their catch – it may have been cold on the Hill Lochs but they've landed 15 brown trout and seem satisfied with that.

Drinks come swiftly, drams all round and a whisky and green ginger for the burly Englishman – Crabbie's green ginger, fire in the belly, a favourite Ne'erday tipple but warming at any season.

The little bar at the Tomich inn is snug, with a fire in the grate blazing up the lum when days are chill. There are pictures round the walls – half a dozen photographs above the bar of grinning fishermen with their trophy catches flopping over their arms or dangling at their side (who caught what and where and the weight of it) and one or two dreamy watercolour sketches of fish, one with a sinuous twist in the mottled back and a languid eye, with a hint of loch shore and an island with a castle on it in the background. In the ingle neuk, incongruously, are two prints of old-time Maidstone. Maidstone? Odd for Tomich, I say, but it seems that's where the landlord lived before quitting the rat race. (He worked in advertising.) Before buying the hotel, the nearest he'd been to the Highlands was Glasgow.

'I'm off for my tea,' says the gillie, finishing his dram.

Later, passing the open dining-room door on my way out, I see, seated at table, washed, changed, brushed, combed and tidied, the burly fisherman and his companion, napkins tucked in at their necks. There's white napery on the table, flowers in a vase, cutlery before them and wine in their glasses. A fine way to round off a fresh spring day in the open.

42

The gillie is called Dennis. He lives at the end of a lane above the road at Tomich.

There are wellies and fishing tackle in the porch. In the tiny living room, his mother brings me a cup of tea. Dennis is a single parent and he and his daughter live with her.

Surely I've seen him before? In Glen Strathfarrar, glimpsed through a screen of alder and birch trees, two people side by side on a shingle bank where the broad river sweeps round noisily. They stood with their backs to me some distance away, a picture of concentration. Dennis – it must have been Dennis – with a net over his shoulder, bent his head to speak to the little old lady beside him. Puffs of white hair fringed the pork-pie hat she wore. She'd a rod in her hand, gave a cast and the line made an arc over the water. I watched for some minutes till they moved on, she teetering over the loose stones of the gravel bed while he laid a supporting hand on her elbow to steady her steps – a respectful rather than intimate gesture.

'Mrs Dunbar,' says Dennis. She's 87, he says, and an enthusiast. He remembers she caught two salmon that time on the Farrar. 'She heard that the Queen Mum caught her last salmon at the age of 89 and she reckons to equal that. Or more.'

'I can't remember when I wasn't fishing,' he says. 'In primary school, if there was a spate, I'd be down at the river right away. I caught my first salmon when I was 11.' His grandfather and great-grandfather were both keen fishermen and the tradition continues. 'My daughter Katy's seven and she started when she was four. She's keen as mustard.' One day she caught 20 trout.

What's the attraction of fishing? 'It's all about the take,' he replies – the split second when the fish takes the fly – 'and suddenly you get this huge surge of adrenaline.' On the other hand, for others, the best sport is when the fish is on the line and they're fighting to reel it in. 'Mrs Dunbar, for one – for her, it's all in the play.'

When Dennis was young, his mentors were the Blue Charm and Willie the Fish (real name Fraser) on the rivers Glass and Farrar. When the Charm advised him to concentrate on one or the other, getting to know every pool and riff and where the salmon lay, he chose the Farrar, concentrating on the lower stretch at Culligran. That's in the latter part of the season. In spring, he's on the Hill Lochs for trout.

'You could put a dozen fish down on this carpet and I could tell you which loch they came from,' he asserts without the hint of a boast, mere matter-of-fact. Well, I'll believe him. Tonight, there are no trout on the carpet, only a box of flies by the hearth. He ties them himself, delicate wispy things, multicoloured, some of them iridescent and glittery. The largest by far, a carroty looking affair, is for catching pike. Among the smaller flies is the one he calls Juliet, named after the wife of Frank Spencer-Nairn who owns the Culligran Estate in Glen Strathfarrar: 'She's very pretty but she doesn't catch a lot.' (He's joking.) In fact, he says, it's one of his favourite flies and, as for the lady Juliet, she's a fine fly-fisher.

Dennis says ospreys often frequent the Hill Lochs. 'Most days you'll see one or maybe two feeding. They've marvellous eyesight. In the last two or three years, there have been sea eagles. There's a good phone signal up there [there's none on lower ground] and, if I see a sea eagle, I text Dan and he comes rushing up.' Dan is the RSPB man who took over from Dave at Corrimony.

Usually, he takes his guests on the loch from nine to five (office hours!) but occasionally they'll go out again at eight, in the gloaming. 'Often you get bigger trout at night,' he says – maybe even five- to eight-pounders, which are weighty fish. These are likely to escape the pot – most of the big ones are dropped back into the water.

Midges can be a torment in late summer. 'I've seen guests with paper bags over their heads and holes cut for their eyes. I've seen guests get out of the car and run to the edge of the loch and push out like mad for the middle. It's usually better out there. But if the wind drops, they'll find you.' He's not affected as much as some but, at the worst, he'll pull a net over his head. He reckons that children are less susceptible than adults – or so it seems with Katy. Loch or river fishing can be equally affected. On the River Farrar, he calculates on losing about four days' fishing a season to midges.

Dennis says that some clients like to be left to fish a river on their own and he'll leave them for an hour or so, returning now and again to check progress. Others prefer his company – his advice and his chat. He's a great talker, is Dennis.

He says that once in late September a stag came down the hill in Glen Strathfarrar looking for hinds.

'I love your Highlands,' said his woman client, an American. 'I've seen a stag and now I can hear a piper.'

'My God,' said Dennis, 'it's my mobile.' (It had a pipe tune as ringtone.) He grabbed it from his vest pocket, it shot out of his grasp and splashed into the pool and, silenced, no doubt lies there still.

43

Every spring six pals come to Tomich from all quarters for a week's fishing on the Hill Lochs. It's the only time they meet.

Forbes, at 80, is the oldest, broad in the shoulder, stocky, slightly stooped, with a quizzical eye. A doctor from Manchester, he has fished in the Highlands for more than half a century. His son played with Dennis at Knockfin when they were boys.

Mark, 40-ish, is the youngest – a detective sergeant in the Met who lectures at Hendon Police College. Like all of them, he came to the sport early. An uncle in Dingwall took him out in a boat, handed him a rod and hey! – he had a bite. In time, he guessed that the fish was already on the line when his uncle put the rod in his hands but he never asked: 'Let me live with my illusion.'

Mike, an engineer, is the heavyweight of the party. The boat settles when he steps aboard. The legs in his breeches are like young tree trunks. He lives in Carlisle where his father was a haaf-netter – wading out into the Solway Firth with a net draped from a yoke on his shoulders like an aquatic Angel of the North. His face is framed by a short grizzly beard.

David's grandfather had a boat on Loch Leven in Fife. David lives in Manchester and travels the world as a consultant in 'enterprise architecture' (I don't know what that means but it sounds impressive). A man for the great outdoors, when young he was a climbing instructor at Glenmore Lodge outdoor centre at Aviemore. He's about to become an alpha-Munroist, having set out to climb every major peak in the Highlands not just once but once in each season. He's on the last lap: 'Eight in summer and seven in winter still to do.'

Howard, a pathologist in Edinburgh, has known this area since boyhood. (He caught his first fish, a perch, in the city's Duddingston Loch.) He spent school holidays with his family in a cottage in Cannich.

Richard, the newcomer to the party, is in business in Suffolk selling kitchens and bathrooms. A chance meeting six years ago led to his adoption by the group.

The catalyst for some of them was Kyle, the man who organises fishing parties on the lochs. 'I wandered into Tomich, was introduced to Kyle and the rest is history,' says Howard. Kyle's eccentricities are legendary. Mike came to Tomich after a planned fishing trip to Ireland fell through. He wrote for information and Kyle's reply was 'so off the wall that I thought, that sounds like my sort of thing'. Mark agrees. Twenty years ago he received a sheaf of glossy bumf about the area, amongst which was a scrap of paper torn from a notebook bearing a badly typed message – the letter e was missing and a heavy hand on the keys had punched holes in the paper. It was signed by Kyle and the significant phrase was 'I liv· and br·ath· fishing'. Mark was hooked.

44

Outside the Tomich Hotel, Kyle is going round 'The Six' with a clipboard, assigning them boats – they'll split into pairs and he and Dennis and another gillie will accompany them. Kyle is a solidly built man, four-square in his black reefer jacket. Greying locks curl under his cap. Kyle manages the fishing for his cousin Donald the circumnavigator.

There are tales about Kyle, a harum-scarum in his youth with a penchant for fast cars. He once sold Maseratis in the Highlands. It's said he mollified the police in France who flagged him down for breaking the speed limit by giving them a spin in his sporty car. This day, he's driving a borrowed all-terrain vehicle and offers a lift up the track to the lochs while the others take an easier route through the forest. He climbs aboard stiffly, grumbling in a rather posh accent (public school, I suppose) about his bad knees and we jolt away. Twice gates barring the way have to be opened. My job.

We park on a grassy patch about a quarter of a mile from the boathouse on Loch a'Ghreidlein, where the others join us. The blue sky is lightly barred with wispy white clouds which cast shifting shadows on brown moorland and dark forest. Blue mountains to the north are splashed with snow. It's cold. Dennis says it was minus two at Drumnadrochit last night.

Out of car boots comes the kit, the rubber boots, the overtrousers, the jackets, the satchels, the whippy rods and fine lines. These reflect individual peccadilloes – wet flies and dry flies are meticulously arranged in Richard's multi-pocket vest, one side wet, the other dry. 'He's a bit obsessional,' Dennis mutters. There's much fiddling with reels and rods raised like lances in the air.

I follow Dennis and his two clients to the boathouse while the others head for the next lochan in the chain, Loch na Beinne Moire. The boathouse, just a wooden hut with a table and a few chairs in it for lunching, is a room with a view. A big window looks north towards faraway mountains. A small cairn nearby is dedicated to 'a lover of the countryside'.

'I once had a man who sat beside that cairn all morning with a bottle of malt whisky,' says Dennis. 'Kyle went up to him and asks, "Are you not fishing, sir? Have you fallen out, or what?"' Not a bit of it. On his first casts of the day the man had caught two big fish, one after the other. 'It was sheer luck of course,' says Dennis. 'Fish were feeding on the surface and he just flicked out his first cast and got a five-pounder, which he put back. He changed the fly and on the very next cast he got another just as big. So he retreated with the bottle and sat there just looking at the hills and swigging.'

'His partner in the boat couldn't have been too pleased,' Mark observes.

'His partner got nothing,' says Dennis.

Mark says he likes to get a couple of nice fish in the boat before he can relax.

What's a nice fish? 'Plate size,' says Dennis. 'In this small loch anything over three pounds is a very good fish.'

As Dennis clambers into the rowboat moored to the jetty, he spots a small insect rippling the water.

'A sedge,' says Mark, scooping it up in the hollow of his palm, where it lies like a small, scrolled-up brown leaf, whereupon Richard produces a lookalike from his pockets and we compare the living insect and the artefact. The similarity is striking.

Dennis says, 'The sedge is the biggest fly we have up here. They normally hatch in June and when they start hatching the fish feed on them exclusively. There's maybe a five-week period when the fish feed on them and nothing else, so that's all we go out with – sedges.'

Mark observes that, since the sedge swam towards the boathouse unmolested, the fish aren't biting. There's hardly a breath of wind and the water's flat calm – not ideal conditions. Nothing dimples the surface.

'We're always trying to fool the fish,' says Mark. 'If the fish thinks it's a real fly in its right environment, at its right depth, at it's right speed, doing the right thing at the right time of year, it'll take it. You've presented an offering to a wild creature and it's accepted it as the natural thing. When you catch a fish that way, you're really hunting.'

The boat edges out from the jetty, Dennis pulling on the oars. The little blue-hulled craft with its bright red gunwale looks a picture on the still water. 'Tight lines!' – it's what you say. Rods are raised in an antic dance, lines flick across the water, invisible flies dimple the surface with a kiss.

I wander across to neighbouring Loch na Beinne Moire, discover the remains of a storm-shattered boathouse grey with age and reached or possibly not reached by a rickety bridge on stilts. Shan't put it to the test. Beyond that, the going gets rough so I turn back to climb little Beinn Mhor again. From its height, I see the blue rowboat motionless in the water and the small figures of Mark and Richard plying their rods with Dennis resting on the oars. No voices can be heard. I see the changing colours of the water, sometimes ruffled, sometimes dead flat, reflecting blue sky and puffy clouds, with the sandy bottom of the shallows showing faintly through. Also the spit of rock named by the Six as Kenzie's Point after Forbes (whose surname is MacKenzie). It's an outcrop of the limestone seam that lies under the lochan and determines the chemical make-up of the water – and even subtly affects the character and taste of the trout that breed there. Or so says Dennis.

From a spot close to the Celtic cross, three of the five lochans are now in view, Loch na Beinne Moire with its distinctive serpentine and fretted shoreline being visibly the largest. At its extremity, a boat is heading for what I make out to be a narrow channel linking it to a further lochan, possibly in hope of finding better luck there – the occupants of the boat are three specks of life in a still landscape of sombre browns.

Five walkers in a row, brightly dressed, came trudging up the track from Guisachan laden with heavy backpacks. They halt near our parked cars, mop their brows, ease packs off their backs and consult maps. I hasten down hoping for a word but, long before I reach the track, they're gone, straggling round the hump of the hill and out of sight, making for Corrimony I guess. A track is marked clearly on the map but on the ground it's a different story, as I know, having once, with Catherine, missed my way through the intervening woodland.

45

Catherine and I are invited to lunch at Tim's. There's home-made pizza and salad served at a table by the open glass doors – Tim, Catherine and I and Tim's wife Alice. The sun's shining and a bee from Tim's apiary is buzzing at an orchid which prompts Tim to remark on the orchid's marvellous efficiency as a receptor of pollination. This leads to a discussion between him and Catherine on moths (her special interest) and then, by a tangent, to the mention of Sir John Lister-Kaye whose home and field centre at Aigas is just along the road to Beauly. He's an excellent naturalist and a great enthusiast, says Tim – we should see him in the field with his clients or students or whatever you call them, where 'he makes a drama of everything'.

Down below us in the field, we see Tim's five brown heifers. He says they often come up to the house and peer through the kitchen window. He talks to them all the time and they follow him. Alice, who lectures in Inverness, says she'd like to have a couple of black cattle of her own when she retires – I think she fantasises about leading them in the cattle ring at the Black Isle showground.

Tim says he and Alice still can't believe their luck in finding this spot for a home. They kept trying to buy old cottages, of which there are plenty in Strathglass in various stages of decay, but no one would sell. Mostly people wanted to keep them in the family. Then they saw ground advertised here at Mauld. When Tim enquired, he was told schedules had already been sent to 300 applicants and one was coming over from South Africa to see the ground, so it looked hopeless. For one thing, they'd no house to sell, having lived until then in tied accommodation. But Tim drafted three short paragraphs describing his background and his plans for the future and it must have struck a chord with the seller – Iain Thomson, a former soldier, shepherd, cattle farmer, now turned author – for his offer was accepted. There was joy when the letter was opened and maybe disbelief. Can this be true?

Tim says four offers higher than his were received so something in those three short paragraphs must have taken Thomson's fancy. They scraped funds together and took a mortgage and here they are. Tim says his early background was not dissimilar to Iain's, which may have helped. He was a stalker in youth and he worked for his father in forestry, besides which he's a great outdoors man, a climber, and he keeps fit. Every year, he does the Highland Cross, the coast-to-coast race between Kintail and Beauly through Glen Affric, running and cycling over the passes.

This time I see his precious old Porsche unwrapped – a dazzling yellow, with an official badge fixed in front of the bonnet that says 'Le Mans Vintage Tour'. He and Alice will drive to France for a vintage Porsche rally later in the year – not to race but to bask in the atmosphere, the sunshine 'and enjoy the food and wine'.

46

By the Abhainn Deabhag burn, near Cougie, a fine morning in June.

In the burn, rather, ankle deep, with George, known to his friends as Darkie because of his black hair and boxer's blue chin. But I shan't call him that.

We splash downstream. The water's low and a bed of round stones like cobbles gleams under the surface in the shallows. Taking care not to slip.

George carries a bucket of water in which a swarm of tiny salmon fry squirm and flicker and dart. He scoops up a ladleful, a dozen or so at a time. Once out of the melee they glitter with an intimate radiance, brassy and spotted on the back with a flash of silver on the belly and just a hint of diaphanous fin. He tips them into the water and they wriggle away, tails flicking as they scurry for shelter among weeds or under stones.

I think of whitebait. Possibly you could pop them in the pan.

We move from shady pool to swift flowing riffle, tipping the fish into the water in penny numbers. Stones roll under our feet.

'No predators about,' says George, looking around. Which is good. These fry would be tasty morsels for any wading bird.

The two- or three-month-old fishlets were collected from the hatchery early this morning. Fingerlings is what Dennis calls them, which is descriptive. When the time comes the young fish, grown to six inches long, will set off on their journey to the sea, with the long drop over the Plodda Falls to negotiate and dams to pass. In two years' time, after a perilous ocean voyage, the survivors will find their way back upstream as grown salmon, when Dennis and his clients and their fraternity stand in wait.

During the rest of the day George and a few others – among them a student, a crofter and the hatchery boss's daughter – stock the burn with as many as a hundred thousand fish, of which only a fraction will survive to face, amongst all the natural hazards overcome, the diligence of anglers.

George tells me that he used to be a water bailiff, patrolling the river on the lookout for poachers. Thickset and burly, his black hair tinged with grey, with a bull neck and black-stubbly jaws, you can see he'd be a daunting figure. One look at him would be enough to make your average poacher give up and come quietly. It's no surprise to hear that he boxed for the army and won money prizefighting at fairground booths.

He has a liking for field sports. He shoots geese on the Cromarty shoreline and, sometimes, crows for a farmer whose crops are at risk. And of course he fishes.

'I shoot nothing that I don't eat'. Except the crows, I suppose. Or does anyone eat crow pie? Country folk used to.

'I catch nothing I don't eat.'

47

High summer and a heatwave. It's been like this for days. They say tomorrow will be the warmest yet.

I'm booked into the backpackers hostel at Cannich where, under a green tin roof, it's oven hot at midday and, by evening, the air is barely cooler. A Chinese girl in the kitchen is preparing a meal for herself and her boyfriend – a simple salad of lettuce, tomato and onion, lighter and more appetising than my heap of spaghetti. But there's a reason for my pasta. The theory is that it will sustain energy tomorrow when needed.

At seven, I phone John MacLennan. 'He's not back from the hill,' says his wife. When I call later, he admits to being knackered – his word – by a long hard day in the blazing sun. Will it be as long a day tomorrow? 'Probably,' says he.

I go for a cooling stroll in the night air and, on my return, find an English couple seated in elderly chairs in the lounge with a bottle of wine between them on the table. I produce another for goodwill. They tell me they're freelance hill guides, here for a few days with a party of 16 Faro Islanders who are lodged at the hotel. They booked by email, sight unseen, and are toughing it out there stoically. Greasy breakfasts are their chief complaint.

Gerald the guide says the Faroese, who count themselves keen hillwalkers, found the two hills they tackled on their first day out a struggle. Perhaps it was their packed lunches – dried cod with whale blubber, he says with wonder rather than distaste. One hill was enough of a challenge yesterday and today they ambled in the Affric woods. We find an atlas in the lounge, look up the Faroe Islands and find the highest hill to be 500 metres at most so they don't get much of a test at home.

They're a mixed bunch of mainly professional people from the different islands, among them a doctor, a teacher and two pharmacists. They get together for an expedition once a year. Gerald says that, before setting off in the morning, they form a circle and sing a chorus and, on the route as the fancy takes them, they'll burst into song. On their second night in Cannich, they danced at the Slater's Arms till half past one in the morning.

I wake early and, at 5.30, I'm sitting at a table in the corner of the lounge writing up my notes in the sooty aroma of the bygone fire in the stove. I have the hostel cat for company.

It rained quite hard in the night, though it barely cooled. As day breaks, the mist begins to lift, parting here and there to reveal patches of blue sky. It's going to be warm again and maybe hotter still.

John pulls up in his 4x4 and points me to the back seat. He has a wary way of looking at me under his brow. In the village, we pick up Chris, who's also a stalker, though mostly he works as a joiner. He and John wear deerstalker hats and tweed breeches in a green check, the standard outfit. 'There's only one gun today,' says John, meaning his client, not the rifle lying beside him in a faded canvas cover. So there will be four of us on the hill.

We park on a grassy patch beyond Fasnakyle Power Station near the derelict kirk and wait for the client to arrive. 'Come on, Andrew,' says John, tapping the wheel impatiently, and at length a car sweeps round the bend in the road and pulls up beside us. Out steps Andrew carrying a six pack of beer which he stows in a cold box at the back of the 4x4 before taking the front seat beside John.

We take the tourist road the length of Loch Beinn a'Mheadhoin then follow the forestry road on the south side of Loch Affric. There's no hint of a breeze to ruffle the glassy surface of the water where trees, rocks and the green and brown hillsides are mirrored in sharp clarity. At the head of Loch Affric, a crescent of yellow sand dips into the dark shallows at the water's edge.

Taking a rough track beyond the head of the loch, we reach the isolated cottage at Athnamulloch. From a shed across the river nearby John brings out a small bug-like vehicle that will take us further up the glen – an Argocat, the standard stalker's vehicle on rough terrain. There's just room for John and Andrew in the cab, while Chris and I go steerage in a kind of tub at the back, seated uncomfortably on hard thinly padded benches. As I climb aboard my hand touches a sticky patch on the rim. There's blood on my fingers and a puddle of blood on the floor – evidence of yesterday's kill.

For several hard miles, we follow a track to Alltbeithe, lurching into potholes and rearing over boulders while Chris and I hold on grimly. Ahead of us John's broad shoulders hunch over the controls.

Alltbeithe is a youth hostel now. The house that stood here is gone, replaced by a timber bunkhouse. People are strolling about outside and we're greeted by the warden, a young woman in a sun top. High hills surround us. John trains his telescope on Ben Attow, a ghostly eminence in the grey haze, and, after an interval, he spots deer high up. 'Moving up fast,' he says. 'Maybe there are walkers about.' Stalkers and walkers are not usually the best of friends but he shows no irritation. It's a neutral comment.

We board the Argocat again and splash across the river, scoring the grassy flats of the valley bottom with tyre tracks before turning into a neighbouring glen in the hope of finding deer on the far side of the ridge. At first, nothing. John, Chris and Andrew silently sweep the tops with their glasses without success until Chris sights a couple of stags on a high crest – but they're too distant to be of interest. I glimpse them briefly, two pinprick antlers outlined against the bleached sky. Eventually, a few beasts come into view below the long high ridge that leads to Ben Attow and we'll go for them.

Before setting out, Andrew and Chris apply plasters to their feet, raw from their long stalk yesterday (Chris was wearing new boots.) John gives each of us a horn-topped stick from the back of the Argocat. Andrew casts off his jacket and I decide to abandon my rucksack as an unnecessary encumbrance. Conscious of the heat, we're walking light – all but Chris who has to carry the gun.

The ground in the valley bottom is boggy but we soon reach firmer ground. The slope is steep, the sun merciless. Ahead of me John slings his jacket over his arm and rolls down his stockings, breeches flapping round his brown calves. A haze veils all the surrounding landscape, softening the sharpest peaks. The sun strikes down, the air is humid. Sweat rolls off John's bald head and runs down his neck. Only an occasional whisper of breeze gives any relief.

We halt, lie flat on our stomachs and gulp mouthfuls of water from a small burn running through the undergrowth. It's a disappointment. The water's tepid, not the ice-cold draught I expected.

We return to the climb, breathing hard, saying little. Sometimes Andrew or Chris is ahead of me but always John takes the lead, setting a measured pace as we zigzag round rock or grassy bluffs taking care to keep hidden from the unsuspecting deer somewhere above us. From time to time, we pause to rest briefly, leaning on our sticks or scooping up more mouthfuls of water.

Finally, John moves ahead on his own, disappearing beyond a rocky bluff to spy out the land. We must be close. No one speaks. John returns and sits on the grass. I watch him take the gun and then five bullets. He slots the last one into the breech and slides the bolt home. He's put on his jacket again.

'Wait here,' he instructs before Andrew and he continue upwards.

Chris and I remain, silent or talking softly now and again. Time passes. Huge pyramids of hill surround us, moody in the light-absorbing haze, all plunging into the narrowing valley called Fionngleann – named, I speculate, after Fingal the Ossianic hero. The Argocat is a black dot far below near the deserted cottage of Camban, a ruin of bare stone walls and green tin roof. Two waters stream down the side of the hill facing us, one a startling dash of white as it drops through a gorge. At the valley floor each turns in an opposite direction – one flows westwards, the other, the Allt Cam-bàn, which is a source of the River Affric, bends eastward on the start of a long journey which will feed its waters, after passage through many lochs and over falls, into the Glass and then the Beauly rivers and finally the North Sea.

Not a sound. The shot, when it comes, is softer than I'd expected, muffled by the bank of hillside between us. 'We'll wait a while,' says Chris. Minutes pass, then another shot and a third. Another pause, then Chris rises and I follow, to find John and Andrew sitting reflectively on the grass. And the stag? John points to a half-hidden dun-coloured rock-like shape a couple of hundred yards down the slope. We move down towards it.

The stag has fallen at a slant, his head bent back – a handsome head, the blue-black eye still moist and lifelike and not yet glazed. We gather round. John kneels, takes his knife, cuts into the breast and slits down the belly. Blood flows and stains the grass. John wrestles the beast on to its back and, as it starts to slip down the grassy slope, he braces his leg against it and calls on me to grab a hind leg. It comes to rest and I feel the dead weight. John thrusts his hand into the belly cavity and drags out the stomach bag, grey and glistening like a dumpling, and then the bunched folds of intestine streaked with a smear of mustard-yellow faeces. They say the beast will have been feeding for body weight in preparation for mating – stags build up their strength before the rut, which is a time of stress during which they barely eat. John's hands and bare shin are bloody, the leg of his breeches is soiled, there's a daub of yellow shit on his hand which he wipes on the grass. He sizes up the animal and estimates its weight at, say, 15 stone.

He makes an incision in a hind leg through which Chris feeds a strap attached to his rope then they lever the body into position for the drag downhill. Chris winds the rope round his stick, which he holds with both hands behind his back parallel to the ground. He braces himself, takes the strain and starts to drag the beast behind him. It's a long way down to the vehicle. John says that, when he was young and worked in Affric with his father, they used ponies – though generally they didn't need to come this far to find deer. We've come many miles to reach this spot. 'Would you like to walk a pony all the way up the glen?' he asks. The Argocat's quicker.

John turns to help Chris manoeuvre the stag for the first and trickiest stage of the drag, telling Andrew to move on upwards. He'll catch up with us later.

We watch them depart, skirting the steeper slopes and dodging hollows, and, in a little while, we find a rocky outcrop where Andrew decides to wait for John's return. It's pleasant to rest in the sun. We chat. Andrew tells me he farms cattle and sheep near Buxton in Derbyshire, selling produce by mail order and on the Internet. Before he came to farming, he was an architect, living in the country but with a practice in London. When a local farmer decided to sell his smallholding of a hundred acres, Andrew bought the land and gradually added more parcels of land to it.

We have a good vantage point. We watch through binoculars as Chris, alone now, diminishes. Halfway down the hill, he strips off his shirt, mops his brow and starts hauling again. There's no sign of John. Half an hour has gone by and he should be back. Where can he be?

He's above us – that's where. There's a whistle – we look up and see him on the skyline, waving. It's not exactly a friendly wave, I think. When we meet again, there's a hint of frost – he's not best pleased, after a strenuous search along the high tops, to find us lounging below like sunbathers. But he's a model of restraint and says nothing. Together we move down the steep irregular ridge, noting as we do so a few deer gathered in a corrie overlooking the neighbouring glen.

We see the tiny Argocat inching forward. 'I hope he stops,' says John and he does. Chris gets out of the vehicle and makes contact by radio-telephone. He's instructed to drive into the next glen and rendezvous with us at a gravel bank beyond the peat haggs.

We move down the ridge cautiously towards the knot of deer, edging off the skyline to avoid alerting them. Once again, John and Andrew continue while I stay. They move over a crest and then, lying on their backs, feet first, heads tucked low, disappear from sight while they wriggle towards the herd below them. It's a tricky manoeuvre. I wait. An arc of sound breaks the silence, an increasing and then diminishing rumble as a plane crosses the clear sky trailing echoes as it disappears from sight.

The shot surprises me. Reverberating round the hills, it seems louder than before. One shot, no more. Wait. Move on cautiously.

I find John and Andrew sitting on a scarp with the deer some way below them at the foot of a sharp drop. Andrew moves first at a half run and we follow. John pulls back the thick hairs on the beast's shoulder to reveal a small red-rimmed orifice where the bullet has entered. It's a good shot, a clean kill.

By now, Chris has moved into the glen and we watch the Argocat splash along by the river. John sets off at speed, the beast slithering behind him. Sometimes he has to dodge aside to prevent it clipping his heels.

Andrew and I ford the river where it shallows while the others load the stag onto the vehicle. Now two stags lie side by side in the bucket leaving little room for the passenger – me. Andrew stands behind the cab, straddling the bench seats, legs flexed against bumps and jolts, scanning ahead like a ship's captain on the bridge. Chris has joined John in the front. I squash in as best I can beside the animals. The journey back is economy class. Bump, thump, jolt, shudder. The late afternoon sun still delivers its hammer blows and a cooling shower of spray is welcome when we plunge into a water-filled hole.

My dead companions lurch heavily against me in a less than neighbourly way. I discover that the hide of a stag, as I try to fend it off, is coarse and hairy. It takes energy to defend my space. A large head with brownish tongue lolling is too close to my face for comfort and the tine of an antler threatens to stab my chest.

Relief comes at last at Athnamulloch, where we transfer to the 4x4. I stretch out on the back seat, pleasantly fatigued. It's been a strenuous outing. 'I'd call it an average day on the hill,' says John. 'You should try it when the weather's bad,' says Andrew. 'Try it in October.'

We take cans of beer from the cool box followed by a dram from the bottle that's been rolling on the bottom of the vehicle. Only now do we think of food, having fasted all day. John produces sandwiches made by Mrs MacLennan, venison soft as butter between thick slices of brown bread, followed by a slab of her home-made fruit cake. A feast.

At Fasnakyle, Andrew speeds away but there's still work to do for John and Chris.

We drive up to the Guisachan steading at Tomich where one of the outbuildings serves as a deer larder. It's a shed with tiled walls and a concrete floor and down the middle runs a drain. Half a dozen carcases hang on hooks – it's like a butcher's back shop – the tally from past days' shooting.

John and Chris sling one of our two stags onto a wooden horse where they cut out the red organs. Then they saw off the antlers and the head, first having prized out the hose-like windpipe. The head is flung into a bucket already half-filled with others. Dark, listless, sightless eyes in a pail.

They weigh the carcase on a spring balance – 15 stone 4 pounds, so John's estimate on the hill was pretty accurate. He takes the saw, cuts down the breastbone, wedges the breast open, sticks a label on the carcase to show the date and place where the stag was shot. The second stag, lighter by a stone, is butchered in the same way. Finally, John and Chris clean knives and saws and hose down the floor and a red river flows down the drain.

48

I wait among pine trees in the last car park in the glen. I'm on the lookout. I have a rendezvous.

A white van with the words 'Forest Research' on the side comes winding slowly through the trees, the red-bearded, freckle-faced driver glancing about him.

'Joe?'

'John?'

We shake hands.

It's August but too early in the morning for the tourists to be about – the bikers, the hikers and the random strollers. We have the forest to ourselves.

We cross the Affric River, dark and still as it flows under the wooden bridge on its way to the great loch Beinn a'Mheadhoin, then plunge into an undergrowth of long grass and straggly heather, the heather bells just beginning to show colour. Who else comes here, off the beaten track, now or at any time? A faint blush of purple is showing on the surrounding slopes. Behind us rears the prow of the lesser Sgurr na Lapaich (two hills in Strathglass share that name), a silent watcher.

The ground is broken and hummocky, the humps festooned with lush vegetation – mosses, blaeberry, cowberry and calluna. We brush through fine-spun, gauzy spider webs, almost invisible, which brush our faces in passing like soft fingertips. A wood ant, bigger and clumsier than the familiar garden kind, flops onto my hand. Joe says old forest like this is its natural home.

We reach a spot in open woodland where, in the near vicinity, a few spreading Scots pine grow alongside a birch or two dripping with hairy lichens, an alder and a spindly rowan. At our feet, a fallen trunk, species unknown, lies felted with vegetation, in slow decay. The remains of a pine tree, which snapped 10 feet from the ground in a winter gale, thrusts up a branch tufted with a single small mop of foliage.

This is Joe's research patch – a sheltered spot in the area marked Pollan Buidhe on the map.

He wanders among the trees, stopping to peer through a lens the size of a thimble, seeking out lichens and mosses lodged in crevices in the bark or drooping pendulously from branches. He hands me the lens and I struggle to focus (there's a knack in it). Suddenly, the blur resolves into a tiny forest of delicate fronds and fluted spicules, a secret landscape emerging from mists. He names this as a species of bryoria, *Bryoria fuscescens* in botanical terms, not by any means a rarity – it's all around. Joe's after something a bit more special.

The morning becomes a lesson in botany. *Parmelia saxatilis* – 'brown branching hairy kind of stuff. It grows on rocks as well as trees. Saxatilis is Latin for growing on stone.' A mass of pale yellowy-green moss draped over a rock is *Racomitrium lanuginosum*, soft and spongy by the look of it but dry and fibrous to the touch. Swathes of *Alectoria sarmentosa* hang from a broken trunk and, close by on a lone pine atop a bluff, *Imshaugia aleurites* – a presumed indicator of woodland longevity. Its presence here helps, in a small way, to reinforce the theory that this pinewood has grown in unbroken succession for centuries and possibly thousands of years.

Elsewhere in Pollan Buidhe, other scientists are busy. Helen is studying what the pollen grains stored in the soil can tell us. With her is Alex. 'I'm the partner,' says he. 'I'm here to help carry the things.'

The sun shines, it's hot, a light breeze stirs the foliage. Pollan Buidhe on a summer's day is a Forest of Arden, except that Shakespeare's Arden never knew midges. Alex, who's small and dark, pulls a gauze veil over his face and trim beard for protection against the tiny bloodsuckers. Helen seems oblivious. I douse myself with insect repellent and we head into the undergrowth.

This cup-shaped hollow in Pollen Buidhe is ideal for Helen's purpose, which is to chart the vegetation that has grown in Affric through the ages. The clues are in the tiny pollen grains preserved for many centuries in the thick layer of peat that lies beneath the vegetation. Here the peat slowly accumulated to a depth of many feet, forming a sink into which a constant rain of pollen fell. Since no stream flushes through the ground the sediment of ages has remained undisturbed and little has seeped away. The picture is clear.

The 'things' Alex helped to carry are mainly a bundle of long tubes. Helen takes the first tube and they screw it into the ground, adding another and then a third as the probe sinks deeper. When the full depth is reached, they withdraw the tubes, now filled with a core of dark peat, a visible record of the past. Each centimetre marks the passage of ten years – a metre's depth is a millennium. Bits of fibrous material survive even at that depth but it's the pollen, invisible to the naked eye, which will provide the information Helen needs.

49

September. Joe's back. His red crop-head pokes out of a window at the Backpackers as I drive up. The Backpackers is where he likes to stay on his field trips in Glen Affric. My cell-like little room (I'm here for one night only) is spartan. It has two narrow beds but no bedside light (a disadvantage for a night reader), a minimal hanging cupboard and no chair. The walls are pale lilac and the thin curtain yellow. But it's cheap and I'm grateful for that.

In the kitchen, I watch Joe cook himself a mess (as in 'mess of potage') of fried sausage and mash. It's somewhat surprising, I suggest, for Joe has a slightly alternative air – I'd expect him to be vegetarian. 'Well,' he says, 'you have to have real food sometimes.' He tells me he's just back from a wedding in Dorset where they roasted a pig on a spit outdoors.

It rains heavily overnight and, next morning, big pools have formed in the gravel yard outside the hostel. Strands of mist cling to the trees and wrap the hills. Grass, heather, bracken and all are sodden but the sun breaks through early as forecast. It'll be hot again.

At the top of the glen, waiting for Joe to return – he forgot some necessary item of kit and had to drive back to fetch it – I take a stroll. Birch leaves backlit by early slanting sunbeams sparkle like cut glass. The foliage is mottled with yellow, a first sign of autumn. Great shags of high heather are in full flower among moss and blaeberry beds. I sit on a stone and enjoy the warmth of the morning sun.

Joe appears – he must have driven like the wind – and we head for another study site in Pollan Buidhe. We're late and hasten up the steep bank recklessly, plunging over wildly uncertain ground. I tumble face down, pick myself up and stumble again. 'You do a lot of falling about here,' Joe remarks.

Sometimes the heather is waist high. A fallen tree trunk has to be circumvented. Deadwood standing or fallen litters the ground in a debris of branches and shredded bark. A mossed-over corrugation in the peat is the earthly remains of a tree long deceased.

Joe finds an insect on his bare arm, a creature that half-crawls, half-hops in sluggish progress, flapping its wings all the time. It's a deer fly, he says. 'They land on the deer, cast their wings and then burrow under the coat where they live parasitically.' (The life of a deer in the wild is not a bed of roses.) He shakes it off.

We reach the study site where pine trees are marked with orange tape and each is identified by a metal disc. Joe stops at a tree perched above a small stony burn to check the number on the disc, takes a compass bearing (orientation is important) and carefully outlines a square section of bark with pins and a piece of string – it's not high-tech. This is his microscopic field of study. The naturalist Edmund Wilson has written that a lifetime could be spent 'in a Magellanic voyage around the trunk of a single tree'. Joe's voyage round this pine tree, picking his way through the channels and creeks in the bark in search of telltale lichens, will be a little less time-consuming.

He identifies several different species of bryoria, adding a caution: 'You have to be careful. Sometimes one species can pretend to be another.' With a knife, he cuts through a little blob on a hairy lichen (of the genus Usnea) and exposes flesh red as a jewel of blood.

Another species catches his eye. This is *Bryoria furcellata*. 'Amazing,' he says. Through the lens, the drab speck springs into vivid detail. It has a fine branching structure, with little spines sticking out like antennae. 'No question,' he says, 'really distinctive, a beautiful specimen.' This is another lichen thought to indicate woodland succession, a hint that the pinewood has had a continuous presence in the neighbourhood, possibly even from the end of the Ice Age.

The downside is that this specimen is growing fractionally just outside Joe's string-and-pin enclosure. It's beyond the pale and won't be recorded. Who'd know, I ask. But Joe, with scientific rigour, won't have it. Furcellata's out.

50

What will the forests of Glen Affric look like in a hundred years' time, in a thousand years, in ten thousand? What changes will there be? Will there be more trees in the future or fewer? Will the mix of species remain the same? What will the landscape look like? These are the questions Joe is attempting to answer in his research for the Forestry Commission. Much depends on variable factors, from fluctuating forestry politics through to climate change.

Joe's fieldwork is only part of the task. The rest he describes as 'heavy maths' (one of his degrees is in maths) and his essential tool is the computer. With so many factors to take into account, the uncertain effect of global warming being only one of them, a layman might wonder where to start. As Joe puts it, 'Gut-wrenching decisions have to be made.'

I visit Joe at the forest research station at Roslin, a leafy place on the outskirts of Edinburgh. Hanging on a wall are maps of the lochs and woodlands of Glen Affric.

I thought the computer screen on his desk would show digitised images of a virtual forest – true-to-life pine trees, birches, hazel, alder, oak and the rest – but no. What I'm looking at is a series of diagrams based on information culled from many graphs and tables, garish and colour-coded like images from outer space, bright red for dense woodland, green for areas of more scattered trees. The computer whirrs and the pattern shifts almost imperceptibly, decade by decade until, over an imagined millennium, the change is dramatic. A thousand years from now, the woodland currently confined to the lower southern slopes of Beinn a'Mheadhoin has spread upwards to encircle most of the hill, with only an island of bare ground left at the summit. Tongues of forest now reach far into the naked glens of West Affric.

This is only one of many projections. It may happen that way or not. Who can tell for sure?

51

At Stirling University, Helen leads the way along a breeze-block corridor to her lab. Helen's time span is not in the future but in the past. She opens an industrial-size fridge to takes out a metre-long core of peat, a thousand-year record of vegetation in Pollan Buidhe. Possibly it was the very core I watched her draw from the ground. The column of peat is notched at two-centimetre intervals where small samples have been extracted for analysis.

She talks about 'pollen rain', the shower of pollen grains that drenches the soil every year with monsoon regularity. Within this core of peat is

Drained of colour in the early morning light – hill and loch in Glen Affric.

Sgurr na Lapaich, distinctive landmark at the head of Glen Affric.

Sunlit islet in Glen Strathfarrar. Impressive stands of Caledonian pines like these descendants of the ancient forest survive in all three Strathglass glens.

ABOVE. Snow-capped Toll Creagach rises to 1054 metres between Glen Affric and Glen Cannich, here seen from a neighbouring height unnamed on the map – hence dubbed by the author No Name Hill.

RIGHT. Sir John Lister-Kaye, writer and naturalist, runs an upmarket field centre at Aigas. Here beside the River Affric he planned a system of woodland paths with the Forestry Commission.

BELOW. Traffic! Bin day in remote Glen Cannich.

Sturdy hill-walkers Bob and Walter relax at the Backpackers' in Cannich. 'You can't go wrong on Mam Sodhail,' they told the author, who followed their advice.

Frank Spencer-Nairn, landowner and deer farmer at Culligran in Glen Strathfarrar, tags a calf, with muscular aid from his farm manager, Hamish.

Colourful collection of flies for the well-equipped fisherman. Will it be Juliet today?

Dennis the gillie rests on his oars on one of the small Hill Lochs, with clients from 'the Six'. Distant Affric hills rim the horizon.

Ex-river bailiff George tips salmon fry into the burn. Few of the thousands released this day will return as adults to spawn after the hazards of their journey to the sea.

Stuart and Tina at the threshold of their home in the woods near Tomich.

Snug's the word for the little house that Stuart built.

John MacLennan – 'Johnny Affric' – with stag. An expert stalker, dressed in traditional tweeds even for a heatwave.

Mosses and lichens encrust a stone near the River Bend in Glen Cannich. Such botanic gardens in miniature flourish in the damp climate of the west.

Louise, a dreamer who smiles at adversity, with Fritz (on the left). Horses are her passion.

Old Duncan – 'Dunky Affric' – nearing his century after a lifetime as stalker, shepherd and gillie, and now author of a fascinating country memoir.

Boris the wild boar and progeny at the trough. All gone to market now.

TOP. Russell, deer stalker for the Forestry Commission, surveys the terrain south of Loch Beinn a'Mheadhoin. But this day the deer evade him.

ABOVE. Shinty match at Cannich. Strathglass under attack.

RIGHT. Sister Petra Clare, 'hermit iconographer', adds a last detail to her virgin and child.

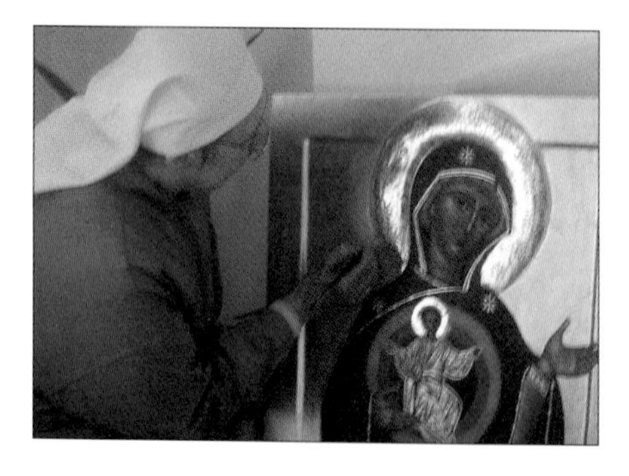

the evidence of a thousand pollen storms. Through the microscope the separate pollen grains swim into view, each species having a distinctive shape. To my eyes, pine pollen has Mickey Mouse ears.

Her project is long term but already one tentative conclusion suggests that, 250 years ago, pine trees in the area of Glen Affric between the head of Loch Beinn a'Mheadhoin and the lower reaches of Loch Affric (including Pollan Buidhe) were sparse, with many fewer trees than grow there now. Most of the ground seems to have been open heath. This is a big surprise. The orthodox view has been that the pine forest has flourished abundantly from time immemorial. The Old Caledonian Forest may have been patchier than we thought.

52

Aigas is a red tower house with a single pepper-pot turret (hence its lopsided look) close to a spectacular reach of the Beauly River. The naturalist Sir John Lister-Kaye, ecologist son of a wealthy industrialist, bought this Victorian pile when it was damp, decaying and neglected and about to be demolished. He had a fight on his hands to save it from the elements and the intransigence of bureaucracy but prevailed against both. From here, he runs a flourishing wildlife holiday centre. Chalets in the grounds accommodate students of all ages, allowing them (as the glossy brochure states) to 'share the wonders of the wild Highlands'.

Nine of us assemble in the drawing room for afternoon tea, settling comfortably in sofas and ample armchairs under the gaze of family portraits and the occasional stuffed creature – eagle, otter or owl. We are granted this privilege because the centre is choc-a-bloc with several groups and accommodation is under pressure. Sharing Aigas this week are school study groups and a large party of visiting American tourists (off to the Orkneys tomorrow and on Sunday, back at Aigas, they'll to the kirk).

Lady Lucy appears bearing a willow-patterned, round-bellied teapot the size of a capercaillie and an ashet piled with home-baked fruitcake. Sir

John, at ease in the window seat, expounds on the treats in store. We shall hear stags roar, see eagles soar and, tonight in the library, there's a wildlife presentation. All this and more we shall see, we shall see.

Next morning we're off to Strathconon, by way of Beauly and Muir of Ord, in a white minibus with a clanking door. 'One of our wildest glens', it says in our notes for the day, but Strathconon turns out to be gentler than the Affric, Cannich or Strathfarrar glens and more populous. There are hamlets and occupied habitations along its length and not a ruinous but-and-ben to be seen.

All day the sun shines.

We turn into the glen and almost at once our eyes are directed to a cottage garden where interesting wildlife has been spotted before. Pencils and notebooks are ready – see that coal tit on the bird table. (Everything is recorded on this outing.)

Shortly afterwards, a small object whizzes past the windscreen. 'Stonechat,' remarks Ieuan laconically, at the wheel. Ieuan, Welsh son-in-law of Sir John, trained and practised as a neurosurgeon until his love of the natural world caused him to switch careers. Everyone tumbles out of the van to watch a pair of red kites quartering a field – great excitement at this demonstration. We disembark again at placid Loch Meig where knowledgeable members of the party point out tufted duck, red-breasted merganser and other aquatic birds I cannot name. I identify two pairs of fishermen sculling in aluminium boats which glint in the sunshine, casting dazzling reflections on the water.

The naming of names continues throughout the day. Frog (common), pied wagtail, dipper bobbing and diving along the river's edge. Black darter dragonflies mating on a blade of grass in a reedy pool, emperor moth caterpillar furry at our feet, bog asphodel on the marshy bank, red-capped fly agaric, a poisonous toadstool, flaunting on a verge. Under plantation trees, Ieuan forages for the yellow crinkled caps of chanterelle which will be his supper for the night.

We lunch on a shingle bank of the Conon River, fine craggy peaks around us. Ieuan sets up the telescope on a tripod, focuses and we take turns to look. The call goes up, 'Deer on the hill' – a herd of hinds with two stags, some lying down, others grazing in a hollow just below the skyline – 17 in all. Soon there's a stir – the deer lift their heads in alarm and suddenly they're up and moving. Dark against the sky a great bird, an eagle, floats into focus, wings outstretched. Oohs! and Aahs! It turns, swoops again and then a third time, and the deer break into a trot that takes them over the skyline and out of sight. Sir John opines that the eagle was trying to harry them towards a cliff edge where a calf might fall and become easy prey.

On the way homeward there's a final show – a pair of sparrowhawks in a dance, and then two kestrels in whirling acrobatics.

'You see this bare hillside?' – Sir John talking.

This day we're in Glen Strathfarrar. A sunny interval in a glade by the river, near Braulen Lodge. We gather round as Sir John expounds. This heather and bracken? These few trees? We see.

It's the cue for a dissertation on how the rich diversity of wildlife in the Highlands has slumped in the past century. This, according to Sir J, is borne out by the old game books for Braulen Estate when it was still in Lovat hands. The game books, shown to him by Lord Lovat, the war hero and dedicated landowner, provide, according to Sir John, documentary record of the natural productivity of Glen Strathfarrar from the turn of the 20th century to World War Two, some 50 years when wildlife proliferated in spite of enthusiastic shooting for game. It appears to have been a golden age which he believes cannot be matched now.

The game books tell of 40 to 50 brace of grouse shot for days in succession, of ptarmigan on the high tops, capercaillie too – the great grouse of the pinewoods rarely seen now but then found in profusion and shot regularly – widgeon, mallard and teal on the river, quantities of snipe on the river flats, salmon for the taking, trout remarkable in size – 'anything from eight pounds and upwards, even a twelve-pounder now and then'. But: 'I haven't heard of anyone catching a big trout, something over four pounds, in the rivers Glass, the Beauly or the Farrar for many years.' As old Dougie, a notable catcher of trout both legitimate and poached, would confirm. Some blame the hydro dams for the decline of river fishing but Sir John believes there are other factors too.

Lovat told him that, as a boy, he had had the freedom of the hills. Too young to take part in shooting with the adults, he and his brother would depart on their own with rifle and shotgun into the woods and hills of Strathfarrar, bringing back mixed bags of wondrous variety. They'd take roe deer, then considered no better than vermin and beneath the notice of the grown-ups, and a wide range of assorted birds including curlew and lapwing – all pointing to a marked decline now in what Sir J calls natural productivity. 'I think the only sensible explanation for this is the very intensive overgrazing by sheep and then deer. Forty years of sheep culture on the back of a livestock allowance which paid people to put as many animals on the land as possible, followed by the proliferation of red deer.' It's well known that red deer numbers have exploded in the years since the war.

Later in the day, near the head of the glen, we wander uphill botanising along a track beside a gully at the bottom of which a small burn trickles. Looming in the west, a presence throughout the day, is the great pyramid of Sgurr na Lapaich lit by the autumnal sun. It looks temptingly climbable. Some other time?

Ieuan points to various heathy things – ling heather with its strong-coloured bells; bell heather with large, paler bells clustered at the top of the stalk; cross-leafed heath with delicate sprays of green spaced around the stem. There are little cries of recognition as the naturalists among us encounter rarities and old familiars – Aha! Devil's-bit scabious. That shy little flower half-hidden in a crevice at our feet, its tiny white petals veined with pink, is eyebright – so named, says Ieuan, because it was used by herbalists in times gone by as a remedy for sore eyes.

Eyebright is duly recorded in our list of the day's finds. Among the birds – stonechat, long-tailed tit, meadow pipit, mistle thrush, hoodie crow. Less confident identification among the lesser creatures – ground beetle, species unknown (a black and yellow bug revealed under a gooey turd-like ball). Even less precisely – 'big black slug'. Clearly there's no slugologist in the company.

Sunday. The Americans, back from the northern isles, are off to the kirk and Sir John summons us to the library for a sermon on stalking. As we gather in the library, I decide not to mention my day on the hill with Andrew and Johnny Affric. Best not to steal Sir J's thunder.

He opens with a question: 'How many are against blood sports?' Two of us raise hesitant hands. Sir John, who has shot for sport and for the pot, nature-lover though he is, declares that, whatever the ethics of the case, deer stalking is important to the economy. It brings cash to Strathglass and the Highlands as a whole.

He produces the tools of the trade: firstly, a three-draw telescope as used by shepherds and old sea salts, then a shepherd's stick, a horn-handled knife with a long thin business-like serrated blade (a family heirloom), a rifle and finally the bullet, small, bright copper-red and jewel-like. This, the death dealer, is split at the nose to flare on impact and maximise the damage. Otherwise it might not kill; might even pass harmlessly (i.e. not fatally) through the flesh.

This is how it goes, he says. Having paid handsomely in expectation of your sport, you arrive at the shooting lodge, which is likely to be spartan, with plain fare probably cooked by the stalker's wife – all the more welcome after a hard day on the hill. If you are a beginner, you will be asked to fire at a target and, if unskilled, may be recommended to practise. And if you then prove to be wildly incompetent, the stalker may decline to take you on the hill.

All being well, you set off. The stalker may carry your gun in its case, the gillie a rope coiled round his shoulders. And you – you carry your lunch box. After a long walk over rough terrain to locate your deer followed by a cautious approach to the herd, the stalker will select a suitable stag and bring you within range while the gillie drops tactfully out of sight. Both you and the stalker wriggle forward on your bellies, heads held low, to within perhaps a hundred yards from the prey. Then the stalker hands you the gun and makes sure of the alignment. Now you have the prey in your sights.

Sir John demonstrates by levering himself awkwardly to the floor – his knees are wonky and he's waiting for an operation. He wriggles forward painfully.

You aim, fire and, if your aim is true, the deer drops. If you wound but don't kill your stag, the stalker will take the gun from you and hopefully despatch it. A clean kill is a matter of professional pride.

Then comes the gralloching. The stalker slits the carcase down the belly and scoops out the innards ('You don't want the stomach juices to spoil the meat.') An image of entrails spilled on the turf, glistening and pudding-like, comes fleetingly to mind as Sir John continues – now the gillie steps forward with the rope to haul the carcase downhill.

We watchers in this drama now follow Sir J outdoors to a nearby field, where he props a thick plank against the bars of a metal trough. This is his target. Meanwhile Ieuan shoos away three inquisitive Highland cattle. Resting an elbow on the gatepost, Sir John takes aim and fires and we move forward to inspect the result. There's a neat hole where the bullet entered the plank and a larger, splintered hole where it exited at the back. We see how the shot, far from spent, carried on to punch through the quarter-inch metal bar behind the plank.

Thus ends the lesson.

Teatime. Coffee, rather, poured not from the china pot but an equally rotund copper kettle.

Laid open beside the tea table there's a small leather-bound volume called *Spicer's Sporting Records* for the season 1913 – a game log for Highland sporting estates 'by Peter Spicer and Sons, Leamington and 60 Academy Street, Inverness, taxidermists by appointment to his imperial majesty the King of Spain.'

Not a good year was 1913. According to Spicer, 'The season will ever be remembered as the worst on record.' The poor bag was 'fully anticipated, as during the cold wet winter hundreds of the deer died on the hills.'

There are references to several estates in our area. At Fasnakyle, where the head stalker was a Mr John MacLennon (*MacLennon*? 'My grandfather,' says John MacLennan), 70 stags were shot, a respectable total – the best weighing more than 19 stone. Seventy were also killed at Benula (head stalker Mr D. Finlayson) but in Affaric Forest (Affaric is an old spelling of the name) the count was a mere 27. At Struy, where 40 stags were shot, the heaviest weighed almost 22 stone.

If 1913 was a bad year, worse followed, whatever the deer count. By the start of the 1914 stalking season, a human slaughter was under way in France and Flanders. It's a fair bet that, by then, many of the younger shooting guests had laid aside tweeds for khaki, some never to return.

Johnny Kingdom comes to Aigas with his TV crew – this man with short curly black hair and a wee bald patch at the back of his head, tattooed arms, talking with a West Country inflection. He lives on Exmoor where most of his wildlife programmes are made and where, he says, it's the custom to hunt deer on horseback.

He and the crew are mostly segregated from the rest of us in the big house. I notice Lady Lucy carrying brown-bag lunches for them with interesting bottles in the bags. We get similar bags but no bottles.

Johnny stands with Sir J on the steps looking out over the grounds, wearing army fatigues and a slouch hat with a pair of feathers in it like Robin Hood. I overhear him say he wants to shoot a stag, with Sir John as his guide. Shocking! Except that he means to shoot his stag with a camera not a gun.

He gets his stag – said that he found the stalk hard going over some very rough ground but eventually a fine stag presented itself nicely to camera. 'I find that they come to you,' he says. I wonder what John MacLennan – Johnny Affric – a stalker of more than 40 hard years' experience, would say to that.

It's five in the morning and dark when we gather in front of the house, still heavy with interrupted sleep. There's a clammy feeling in the air, mist clinging round ghostly treetops. No one talks much.

We rendezvous in Corrimony with Dan the new RSPB man. Dan's a Geordie, a broad-built man dressed in tweed breeches and green wellies. It's going to be wet underfoot, he says. And some of us, foolishly, are wearing trainers.

The morning mist begins to dissipate as we reach the moorland and, in the half-light before dawn, we see a few blackcock. It's not yet the season for the lek. They're not in the mood. What we hope for is to hear the roaring of stags, which have been elusive so far. Dan says we might even hear the screeching of sika deer, the Japanese species introduced into Britain some time ago and now spreading throughout the land and present here.

All's quiet except for the plod and splash of feet over marshy ground. There's no path through the heather and we spread out, trying to avoid the sloughs and finding a route as best we can. Those wearing trainers fare the worst. Heathers laden with water droplets brush our legs, soaking trouser legs and infiltrating boots.

Dawn breaks, the sun tipping the horizon. The hills of Affric, Cannich and Strathfarrar are blue in the distance above billows of white mist. Loch Comhnard's a shining disc below. We gather on a small rocky outcrop with a wide view of the surrounding countryside. Dan says that deer often gather around the channel of the Enrick River about half a mile away but its grassy lawns are untenanted this morning.

'Listen,' he says at last and we all strain our ears. Sure enough, from a region of dark plantation trees still smoky with lifting mist, comes a faint sound of – what's it like? Snoring? – a stag giving voice a long way off, a mournful sound under the vault of the sky. Again it sounds and then again and then silence. We wait in vain for a repeat performance. Perhaps it's too early in the season. Late September it may be but the stags aren't roused to the full passion of the rut. October's the best time.

We troop back to the van, with the rising sun warming our backs, well satisfied to be out of doors in the wilderness under a cloudless sky and ready for breakfast deferred.

53

Notice at Tomich Post Office:

> National Moth Night!!!! [four exclamations] Saturday. Learn about the beautiful insects that fly in your garden each night . . .We will be running light and sugar traps on the reserve until 10 pm . . . All moths will be returned unharmed once identified. Donations welcome.

I phone Catherine: 'You should be here.'
'It's moth night everywhere,' she says.

54

The little yellow wooden café is gone. Not a trace of it today as I make my way south through Glen Urquhart.

It was long in the going.

Once, on my way home from walking in the pinewoods of Glen Strathfarrar, I stopped there and sat by a sunny window with a cup of coffee and a slice of home-made apple tart on a plate. I talked amiably with the couple behind the counter, a black-haired Englishman and his blonde wife, and made a mental resolution to return on my next visit to Strathglass. I never did. When I next passed that way, the yellow paint was flaking, I could see the chairs and tables stacked higgledy-piggledy inside and the café was closed, never to reopen.

A pile of paperbacks was stacked on the counter beside the cakes and scones. The cover showed a young fresh-faced, dark-haired man crouching on a hillside cradling a lamb, with his shepherd's stick across his knee and two collie dogs at his side. The title was *Isolation Shepherd* and the author Iain R. Thomson, a name I didn't know. According to the blurb, it told of the author's shepherding days at the far end of Glen Strathfarrar in the 1950s. I bought a copy and started to read.

It opened: 'A south westerly gale and heavy showers swept down Loch Monar. It had been blowing and raining since the previous day. Though summer storms are not infrequent in the high hill country, this one was severe . . .'

Aboard a small boat on the choppy waters were Thomson, his wife Betty, their two-year-old daughter and week-old baby son, along with their household effects piled under a tarpaulin.

> Head on she met the full force of the weather in the wider open waters. Her cargo that day was my family and flitting, destined for a new home, six and a half stormy miles westwards . . . cradled in remoteness and grandeur at the upper reaches of Glen Strathfarrar.

They reached their cottage safely, found the fire already lit and ablaze, hung their wet clothes to steam at the hearth and made a simple supper. Outside, the sky cleared – a cue for the author to turn lyrical: 'That night we unrolled the mattress on the floor and lay listening. Only the note of the burn and the catching voice of the wind on Creag na Gaoith sang the last of a summer's storm.'

I took the book home and finished it at a sitting. Since then, it has fallen apart through frequent thumbing and I've bought a fresh copy – it's still in print. Over time I heard more about Iain Thomson – that he'd farmed cattle in Strathglass, that he'd turned his hand to writing, and above all that he'd featured in a film about his strath and these glens made for television years ago. Apparently it was made by a man called Mickleburgh who lives somewhere in the area. Clearly, it's a film I ought to see.

From the village of Drumnadrochit, hairpin bends wind up to the moorland above Loch Ness and here I find a low house, part old and part new, that rambles this way and that so confusingly that it's a puzzle to find the entrance. Lawns, trees and shrubs transform cottage garden into a miniature park.

In the kitchen Edwin Mickleburgh introduces the woman standing at the table as Sue. She has her coat on. 'Sorry,' she says, 'I have to leave. There's lunch on the table'. And with that she goes.

'Your wife?'

'My third,' says he.

On the sideboard, prepared by Mrs Mickleburgh III, are plates of cold ham, cheese and tomatoes and a bottle of Chablis, chilled and uncorked.

Lunch consumed and glasses drained, we settle in the lounge to watch the video. The title, *An Element of Regret*, appears on the screen, introducing a two-part film made for Central TV, one of the early television companies, long gone. Edwin says that the documentary changed course halfway through filming. It was conceived as a celebration of the Affric pinewoods until a chance meeting with Thomson in the bar of an Inverness hotel persuaded him that the former shepherd had a better story to tell. It was two years in the making, a generous schedule that wouldn't be feasible now.

The film opens moodily with shots of dark clouds sweeping over the hills and the play of many waters in the glens, with a slow, gravelly voice hymning the allure of wilderness places. Cut to a gentler scene – a sunlit stretch of loch cleft by the bow-wave of a launch. In the stern stands Iain Thomson in his prime – hawk-like features, tanned cheeks aglow, talking of the years he spent at the head of the loch a decade and a half before the film was made (so we're in a double time warp).

'I turned my back on civilisation,' he says on screen. 'I found myself there.'

There are cameo appearances by the locals. John MacLennan's father, in ruddy health, with the same wee deprecating smile I recognise in his son, talks about stag shooting and the importance of a swift despatch: 'For the sake of the animal and for the sake of the gentleman, there's great satisfaction when you have a clean shot.' Donnie, veteran stalker on the Culligran Estate, uneasily contemplating his boss's intention to farm deer like cattle: 'I wouldn't like it,' he says, imagining a slaughter of captive beasts.

Clips from the archive include a black-and-white Ministry of Information documentary made just after the war extolling the grand hydro-electric schemes then being planned or already under construction throughout the Highlands. Scenes from an unidentified location show huge mechanical diggers scooping out rock and earth to the accompaniment of an enthusiastic commentary. Cascading burns are dismissed as 'running to waste' or elicit breathless admiration: 'See that spate of water – that's *power*!'

Iain Thomson has another take on it – that the coming of hydro-electricity wrote the final chapter of the Highland clearances. He and his few neighbours were displaced to make way for the rising waters. 'The hills are sad for the old days and they won't return,' he says. (A poetic fallacy – the hills are indifferent.) Shots of Iain's doomed croft house at Strathmore underline the message – stripped bare, surrounded by tilled fields beside a calm inlet of the old loch, it's an empty shell with flames leaping from the rafters.

Pait Lodge, once home to Iain's nearest neighbours half a mile across the loch and built on higher ground, still survives as a bolt-hole for a south-country laird and his guests. In the film, two elegant cars, one an open-top tourer, wind slowly along the narrow road towards the Monar Dam, where the occupants emerge, women in slacks, men in country casuals, chattering in cut-glass accents. It could be a picnic, with hampers and champers. The party sails down the loch before disembarking from the launch at Pait landing stage for their stay at the lodge. Hampers are unloaded. A lady hands a bunch of flowers for the gillie to hold while she steps ashore, to his clear embarrassment. Inside the lodge, the table is set, sparkling with crystal and silver, with napkins folded, glasses in place and candles lit.

'It's a great place to relax,' the gentleman says to camera.

Far from Pait Lodge and his personal wilderness in Glen Strathfarrar, Colin Stroyan resides for much of the time in an old house in rural Perthshire. There's a row of bells in the kitchen for summoning servants but those days are gone. His wife greets me at the garden gate with a trowel in one hand and a punnet in the other and takes me inside to Colin – a tall man, genial, heavily built and now a bit slow on his feet.

Stroyan is laird of West Monar and Pait, which together cover 35,000 acres of bare hill and moor straddling the top end of Loch Monar. He never saw the loch before the dam and likes it pretty well as it is. He bought the land not long after the great inundation, knowing that the family estate in Perthshire was destined to pass to his elder brother (Harrow and Eton, a judge on the English circuit, recreations field and country sports). As for himself, he spent a lifetime in legal circles in Edinburgh as a Writer to the Signet, a rather grand category of Scottish lawyers, acquiring a clutch of directorships on the way.

A painting on the wall shows a shooting party setting off for the day's sport against a backdrop of loch and blue hills – a lad in the forefront leading two ponies followed by younger versions of Stroyan and wife, tweed clad and striding out along the track beside a brawling burn, with stalker and gillie in the rear. In the background, Pait shooting box is screened behind a clump of trees.

The lodge and keeper's cottage beside it are all that remain of the former habitations that existed around the head of the natural loch. Stroyan had a causeway built to the lochside, demolished two outbuildings and made various improvements to the lodge but stopped short of putting in electricity – which is ironic, considering that the sole purpose of the dam was to provide hydro power. But dark nights are aglow in the soft lamplight. (A generator provides electricity for the keeper and his partner in their cottage.)

These days, Pait is a summer residence. Colin Stroyan sails up the loch to open it up in April and, from then until mid October, the family and friends enjoy country pursuits in comfortable isolation.

Deer stalking and fishing are his passion – his face lights up when he reminisces about sporting days. In his heyday, 12 hours on the hill kept him fit. What gives him his greatest pleasure now? His answer surprises – it's the vicarious thrill of seeing a novice get his (or her) first stag. He shot his first at the age of 11, more than 70 years ago, and he says that, even now, he could find the spot.

Colin Stroyan is not a fan of Iain Thomson, whose home was just across the bay from Pait. 'He was only there a few years,' he says but I guess shepherding at the far end of Loch Monar, with a wife and young family to provide for, might teach something about the nature of the place.

'The book's a good read,' say I.

'Oh, yes, a good read . . .'

55

First sight on turning into Iain Mackay's croft house near Beauly is a shed with strings of onions dangling at the open doors. He's an organic grower. Dung's the thing.

Iain Mackay was Iain Thomson's nearest neighbour. He and his brother Kenny got no compensation for losing home and occupation when the waters rose – unlike the laird, their employer, Sir John Stirling. The sum Sir John received was never made public. Whatever it was, no doubt it softened the blow.

Sir John studiously avoided contesting the Monar hydro plan when it went to a public inquiry. Emma Wood, in her book *The Hydro Boys*, quotes him as saying later that he 'was not at all pleased at this ruination of [his] property' but that he 'had to accept the views of the powers that be that it is a good thing to have all this power developed'.

Three lairds shared the Strathfarrar lands at that time – Stirling, Lovat and Sir Robert Spencer-Nairn, owner of the Culligran Estate and the only one to oppose the scheme at the inquiry. He had been assured by Tom Johnston, Churchill's wartime Scottish Secretary and by then mastermind of the Highland hydroelectric schemes, that Monar would never be dammed in his lifetime but he survived into his 90s and saw it happen.

Tom Weir put in a word for the mountaineers who were about to find the hills harder to reach. Iain Mackay also appeared at the inquiry, armed with a petition from family and neighbours – 12 signatures in all, a paltry number as it might seem to the wider world but, in fact, one hundred per cent of the resident population. During the inquiry, he was asked to ferry the presiding QC and other interested parties on a fact-finding mission up the loch on a January day with a fresh wind blowing. Not far from the shore, these less-than-hardy souls decided they had seen enough and turned back.

Iain Mackay moved down the glen. He never married and lived with his sister until her death. Apart from his crofting, he has dabbled in various interests. On his travels around the country as a stalker for the old Red Deer Commission, he hawked Iain Thomson's book to shops and cafés on the way – including the yellow café where I first saw it.

He shows me a book about the flooding of the glen, which he wrote and published himself, called *The Last Highland Clearance*. The front cover shows two contrasting photographs taken from the same point near the site of the dam. One shows 'the farm at Monar' before the dam was built. There are level green fields in the foreground bisected by stone walls and ringed with clumps of trees, beyond which stretches a serpentine twist of blue loch at the foot of hills, with a farmstead in the middle distance. The second act is starker. The loch has swamped fields and trees and its grey surface (on a dull day) fills the lower half of the picture. The raised shoreline, which formerly shelved gently to the water's edge, is now a grey bathtub ring and the bare hill above it is bleak.

Mostly, it's a book of pictures – images of then and now – and more polemical than most of that genre. Of the latter-day views, only one shows to advantage – a shot of Pait taken in a rosy twilight with a small boat moored at the edge of the placid loch. For the rest, the overriding feeling is a sense of loss. Only a few remnant trees above an eroded scar on the hillside remain after the flood, contrasting with the former scene – a handful of dwellings by a roadway, smoke rising from the chimneys, cattle grazing at the waterside. A man, identified as Willie MacLennan, leads his ponies along the road above his home near Benula Lodge – house and road now submerged and the people gone. Fire gleams behind empty windows and flames leap from cottage roofs as the settlement at Strathmore is put to the torch in preparation for the flood.

A passage in the text tells an even more eloquent story than the pictures. It's an extract from a letter to Iain Mackay on the death of his mother. The writer, a man called Nettleton, had passed by Pait on a trek through the area when he was a young man waiting to be called up to the army in 1940:

> I took ten days' holiday and travelled up north for the first time from my home near London. I packed my rucksack and set off crossing Glens Garry, Morrison, Affric, Cannich, Strathfarrar, Strath Bran, Fannich and Strath Dirrie. I spent two days at Benula at the head of Glen Cannich – this beautiful area was a hive of activity.
>
> On my way over to your old home at Patt [*sic*], I got a welcome cup of tea at Lungard right at the head of the glen and again at Patt, from your mother. I was offered a boat run across to Strathmore but declined as I wanted to walk all the way and to see the marshes and meadows at the head of the loch. I found a dry hillock and got into my sleeping bag and spent the night listening to the constant cries of [waterfowl] and after a beautiful sunrise the chorus was increased by the blackbirds and thrushes in the woods at Strathmore and Patt answering each other across the loch. On getting up at 6am I found a greenshank lying on her eggs less than twenty yards from where I had slept – it was a night and a morning I will never forget.
>
> It was well over forty years later I decided to do the same walk again.
>
> Beautiful Benula has completely vanished from the face of the earth and I had some extra walking to get round to what was once the head of Loch Lungard. Patt lodge was still there and a small replacement house but everything else, including much of the wood, is gone. Strathmore and its woods are completely obliterated

> and the thousands of birds seem to have vanished. I had miles of extra rough walking to get round the head of the loch. Beautiful Strathmore glen with all its meadows marshes and islands is now hundreds of acres of stinking mud. On my first visit there were dozens of small black duck on Loch Monar. This time I could see none.

This chimes with Emma Wood's comment in *The Hydro Boys*:

> Loch Monar was one of the most important places in Britain for moor and waterfowl. Teal, widgeon, redshank, greenshank, curlew, snow bunting and lapwings were only some of the regular visitors to the loch before the creation of the reservoir destroyed their habitat.

She comments that today the dam builders might have a harder fight on their hands.

But would they lose? The naturalists, the conservationists, all those who cherish our wilder landscapes may speak with a louder voice than in the heyday of the old Hydro Board but green energy is big business today with plenty of industrial muscle and political influence behind it to promote its case.

The Monar Dam in Strathfarrar was the last of the great 20th-century hydro schemes in the Highlands. Fifty years later, the *Herald* newspaper carries a front-page headline in large type 'Hydro is back as waters rise behind new Highland dam', referring to a new hydroelectric development at Glendoe which creates a huge new loch in a remote stretch of Inverness-shire moorland where no loch has existed before. Scotland's first minister Alex Salmond is pictured in hard hat and yellow oilskins, with a heap of spoil behind him and brown water gushing from an outlet as he opens a sluice to let the floodwaters in. His enthusiasm echoes Tom Johnston's half a century earlier that enough electricity would be generated in Glendoe to power a city the size of Glasgow – 'Hydro is back!' On that day, it is also reported in another column that a survey has identified one thousand potential river sites in Scotland for small- to medium-scale hydro projects.

In his letter to Iain Mackay, the wanderer Nettleton, older and wiser, concluded sadly: 'My first walk was the eight most wonderful days of my life and the last walk the saddest and most depressing.'

'An element of regret' – the title of Mickleburgh's film and a straight lift from Iain Thomson's commentary – is not absolutely a ringing condemnation of change. In another scene from the film, you see Iain Thomson standing at the bar of the Cnoc Hotel reflecting on a way of life obliterated by the rising tide: 'It's hardly possible to keep people quaint for the benefit of tourists.'

56

Lights are bright in the Inverness bookshop. There's a crowd, people with a glass in hand or browsing the shelves, one or two even reading. And there's music from fiddle and accordion.

I take a dram, I buy the book *The Endless Tide*. On the blurb, these words: 'Iain R. Thomson currently lives near Beauly. He is well known all over the Highlands. From farm servant to the Royal Horse Guards to cattleman for a Russian cattle baron, his life has been rich in extraordinary incident.'

Here in the bookshop on a blustery winter's night, he's in his element, holding court, now darting here and there to greet friends, now seated at a table with a stack of books at his elbow, pen in his hand and a line of buyers queuing for his signature, which he dashes off with a flourish. A tall, lean, rangy man with a beaked nose and a head of grey hair, wearing countryman's check breeches, green stockings, polished brown brogues, his sweater sleeves rolled up to elbow. The speech he makes is like his book, a headlong rush of anecdote and yarn told with gusto.

The entertainment continues. A small wisp of a man, a prizewinner at the Mod, sings a wistful Gaelic ballad in a lightsome voice. Then Iain slings an accordion round his neck, the fiddler joins him and they make energetic music. We should have danced.

There's no one I know among the guests (a surprise) but I chat with one or two: a woman of a certain age wearing lime yellow trousers and jazzy waistcoat and a tall farmer with a fine head of flowing hair, leaning on a shepherd's stick, who tells me he's one of the DC Thomson publishing clan in Dundee – 'the *Beano* and the *Dandy*', as he says.

The Herald has sent me a copy of *The Endless Tide* for review. Here's an extract:

> In the course of his life Iain R Thomson has been variously shepherd, cattle farmer, agro-politician, deep-sea yachtsman, jack of all trades, reveller, and latterly something of a philosopher-poet . . . Here, zestfully told, are tales of rubbing shoulders with the great and the good, Margaret Thatcher for one, and – more to his liking – the Queen Mother, of boisterous nights with cronies in the Castlebay Bar on Barra; of the perils of transatlantic crossings under sail and a flood of gripping adventures in small boats sailing around the Western Isles.
>
> Born the son of a sea captain, fascinated as a boy both by tales of seafaring and by the drama of the cattle ring, he opted out of formal education – 'Goodbye school . . . bye-bye college' – and got himself hired as an 'orra loon' on a north-east farm in the days when there were people in the fields and the horse was king. Thereafter he spent several years as a young man, with wife and small children, shepherding in one of Scotland's remotest glens.

A short quotation from the book captures his prose style in full flight (he's describing the Viking longships): 'Graceful, buoyant as a feather, they skimmed the sea, flexing to the waves, breasting a shoulder, swooping through a trough as a fulmar will at the merest tilt of a wing.'

He's an incurable romantic – but shrewd too.

57

I meet Iain from time to time – in the caravan where he writes, in the bar at the Cnoc Hotel and now, with Catherine, in the Lovat Arms in Beauly. Iain, in his 70s, still has an eye for the ladies and he and she get on famously.

He's been fascinated with cattle and sheep since he first saw them in the ring as a boy. Later, when he quit the army, his CO was astonished that he should choose to abandon life as a guardsman for the mud and muck of the byre. For Iain, it was the taste of freedom. Shepherding at Strathmore at the head of Loch Monar gave him his chance. The remoteness and self-sufficiency of life there, as chronicled in *Isolation Shepherd*, were liberating. 'I loved being on my own, far from interference,' he says. And: 'As soon as I go north I'm a happy chap.'

With the pride of an expert, he's scathing about a TV programme which purported to tell how the cattle drovers of previous centuries led their herds from the Highlands to their markets or trysts in the south. Authenticity vanished when the supposed drovers couldn't get their beasts across a river. The cattle stood on the bank stubbornly refusing to enter the water. What you do, he says, is you take a calf, sling a noose round its neck and haul it into the water behind a boat by main force. 'It's half strangled, its tongue lolls out, it bawls – don't tell the RSPCA. The mother follows, of course, and then all the others.'

Another tip – how to bury a dead bull in a field. The point of the awkward operation (a bull is a ton weight or more) is to ensure it doesn't end up in the hole on its back, otherwise its feet will stick out of the ground. This is history, of course. You wouldn't be allowed to do it now.

He tells how he came to figure in *An Element of Regret*. The film had originally focussed on the pinewoods of Glen Affric and Finlay Macrae, the bearded, pipe-playing head forester there. It happened that the director Edwin Mickleburgh chanced to overhear Iain in the bar of an Inverness hotel telling a friend about his time as a shepherd. He had a few words and a drink or two with him and hired him on the spot. And so, in a sense, Iain poached the leading role while Finlay, from what I've heard, was less than pleased.

Iain again. The talk turns to graves. 'I happened to have some cash and bought a stone,' says he. He had it erected in Struy kirkyard 'to honour the memory' of his forefathers, and his own name is already carved on it too – 'all except the dates'. It stands beside the little kirk, a tall plain black stone incised with a long list of names, among whom are: Hector Mackenzie Fraser, inspector of the poor, Iain's great-great-grandfather; Hector Fraser, master mariner SS *Tiranu Maru* (great-grandfather), 'went down with his ship Liverpool bay October 1918'; Hector Fraser Thomson, master mariner (father), SS *Brittany Coast*, port commissioner Valetta, Malta 1942; Iain Robert Thomson (himself), farmer, Strathglass [no dates as yet] and his son Hector Fraser Thomson, 'killed in Teanassie burn 3rd March 1971, aged 15'.

Iain remembered young Hector on the last page of his second book *The Long Horizon*: 'I hurt my back pulling a plough at the mouth of the shed. Hector stayed off his studies to help. A hard day for a boy . . . Above the Teanassie burn the fence wires were cut and he fell.'

58

'Best to meet early,' said Sheena, Iain Thomson's daughter, so I'm on the road at seven. On the way, a stag leaps in front of the car from a high bank on the narrow back road to Struy. On and on, it runs ahead, a Landseer monarch not at bay but sadly out of its element. Best to leave plenty of room in case he turns – which he does, suddenly. He rears up and I jam on the brakes, at which he skids ungracefully, bellyflops on the turf then staggers to his feet, clears the fence with a bound and is last seen heading across the flats towards the river in a lordly scamper.

Sheena won't be pleased to hear about this. She's just won a battle to have the deer fenced off from her ground and here's one back.

No one's about at the steading, a long stonewalled building with the little white caravan where Iain writes his books parked at the side. It's he who turns up first in an old red car. 'I didn't know you were coming,' he says. 'Have a cup of tea. Sheena won't be here for half an hour.' And he disappears into the caravan. No sooner said than she arrives and, not intending to waste a minute (there are a hundred large beasts to feed), she starts the day's work and my mug of tea is left untasted.

Most of the cattle are a cross between Aberdeen Angus and Salers, a French breed – 'Good ranching cattle,' she says, which means they're hardy and happy in the Scottish outdoors, and good milkers too. The Aberdeen Angus connection adds a premium to the beef price.

When Iain quit farming, he sold his cattle to his daughter to start her off. ('She got them at a good price,' he says later, sotto voce.) Now, since her partner died, he helps out. He says she's a good cattlewoman.

The bulls are fed first: Sean, Jack, Strathglass Oakleaf and Indiana Jones, three with the black sheen of Aberdeen Angus, one red-rusty – the Salers. Sean the Aberdeen Angus has a ruff of black curls on the nape of his neck – he's handsome and valuable too, £3,000 worth of muscle, bone and beef. Among the females, one, a 17-year-old grandmother to a good number of the younger generation, is clearly a favourite – she gets a kindly word and a pat on the ragged rump in passing. She's out to grass, sure of her keep for her natural life. She'll never find a place in the food chain, that's for sure. But, in any case, since she was born before BSE, mad cow disease, a cut of her rather stringy rump would be illegal eating.

A bull down the lane bellows loudly as we approach. 'Just saying hello,' says Sheena reassuringly.

Then she manoeuvres a tractor out of the shed and I perch on a wheel casing while she spears a bale of hay on the forklift and we trundle down the road with the bale hoisted aloft. She grumbles that these big tractors weren't designed for women – she has to stretch to reach the pedals and the gears aren't easy – but she drives it like a dodgem all the same. Meanwhile, Iain emerges from his caravan, mounts his bike and pedals off ahead of us.

Sixty cows and their calves await us in a compound. As the tractor noses through a welter of heaving black backs and Iain stands on the trailer shovelling out pellets of feed, the cattle close in behind us, jostling for a place at the trough. Iain jumps down among them, whacking and prodding with his stick to make sure all get a share.

Back at the steading, we swill muck off our boots in a burn and Sheena announces that she'll be spending the rest of the day spreading muck. I opt out of that to join Iain in his poky caravan. There's barely room for the two of us to sit at the table among a litter of books and papers including a fading copy of the *Financial Times* two months old. There's also a diminutive stove and a fridge for the milk. Iain puts the kettle on and gives a stir to the pan of porridge plop-plopping on the ring. This time I'll get my tea.

'I wrote two books here,' says he. And he's just finished a book of poems which he doesn't 'suppose anyone will publish'.

There doesn't seem to be a handle on the door. 'Kick it,' he says, which I do and it swings open.

His parting words: 'Give me a call next time and we'll have a pint.'

59

John MacLennan comes to the caravan park at Cannich. It's evening, dark and misty, and I go out to the gate to guide him in. A full moon shimmers through the trees – ghostly.

I pour him a glass and talk about his father Old Duncan and how I saw him in the film *An Element of Regret*. Duncan, in his middle years then, was talking about the ethics of stalking and the satisfaction in a clean kill for both stalker and 'the gentleman'.

'Would you talk about "the gentleman" nowadays?' I ask.

'Not at all,' says John. Such barriers have been broken. 'In the old days stalkers were never on first-name terms with the guest. It was always "Sir". But that's all gone.'

Names . . . In those days, he says, when red deer were fewer in number and the sport was not so commercialised, stalkers would know their stags by name. No longer.

Stalkers were hired in the spring and, before the shooting season they were sent out to collect the antlers shed on the hill, just to keep a check on numbers. A stalker might be sent out to kill a particular stag and, if he didn't succeed, he'd think nothing of coming back empty-handed. It's not so now.

As John speaks, his father comes vividly to mind, reminiscing by his fireside about the old days. 'If a stag ran off you took your hat off to him,' he told me. 'That's what I'd call sport.'

John says that a bit of ground on every estate was kept as a sanctuary where the stags were left in peace till they came out to the hinds at the rut. They'd be fed regularly on maize and locust beans which kept them in the sanctuary. These days, especially with so many hillwalkers about, the stags keep on the move.

This is all unknown territory to me. What if I had a stag in my sights, I ask (an unlikely event), where would I aim – at the head or the heart?

Wrong on both counts. John says the best place to shoot a stag is the chest area behind the shoulder – 'the boiler house where the vital organs are'. Talk of a heart shot is a fallacy. The heart isn't big and it's low down. The head's out too, mostly, unless you're aiming from behind at the back of the head. 'There's a good chance of only breaking the jaw if you aim at the head and the stag would be off with a cruel wound and die of starvation.' And John wouldn't favour a neck shot unless you're within a hundred yards of the quarry, aiming fairly high on the neck to make sure of severing the spine.

If I really want to know about stalking, he says, I should read the book *Deer Stalking in Scotland* by Kenneth Whitehead. I think I might.

John says that he started stalking full time in April 1965 when he and his father were working with ponies. That lasted until about 1969 when vehicles took over, allowing stalkers to penetrate further into the hills. In those days, his father would come up the loch by boat. 'There are places where I stalk now he was never on.'

Now, after more than 40 years on the hill, he reckons he's got about five years to go. It's the end of a tale. There will be no more MacLennans – with or without a 'gentleman' – in Affric.

60

Deer Stalking in Scotland, as recommended. A primer (published 1964), short and easy to read – even the technical bits (muzzle velocities etc.).

Sometimes Whitehead chuckles.

> If during a crawl you happen to be following your stalker but carrying the rifle yourself, be certain to see that the safety catch is on and the barrel is not pointing up your stalker's backside. For this reason stalkers generally prefer to carry the rifle themselves, only handing it to the gentleman [gentleman again, in the 1960s] when the firing point is reached.

Also: when aiming at a stag while lying on your back with the barrel pointing down your legs, don't shoot yourself in the foot.

Sensible words, too, on the question of what to eat on the hill. Nothing elaborate – 'a few sandwiches – preferably meat – and a piece of slab cake with perhaps an apple or an orange, easily carried in the pocket. Tomato sandwiches should not be included, for when squashed, the whole becomes a soggy mess.' This I know from experience.

Whitehead remarks that 'whisky is best left at the bottom of the hill'. Wise.

61

Stormy last night, with wind and rain. Came a thump in the night on the caravan roof and I rose from bed bare-legged to investigate, opened the door half expecting to find someone there but saw only inky darkness. I conclude that a branch from a pine tree has landed on the roof and go back to sleep.

Walk down the road for a paper in the morning. Caught in a drizzle but encouraged at breakfast by a hint of brighter weather. Sure enough, the sun breaks through on my way into Glen Cannich.

Near the top of the hairpins above the village, I see four men peering into the undergrowth at the roadside. They don't look like locals. One carries a couple of plastic bags, bulging and knobbly with stuff inside. Gathering mushrooms, I think, to sell round the hotels and restaurants.

The river comes into view as I reach the top of the pass and start my descent into the glen. Through a screen of riverside trees, out of the corner of my eye, I catch sight of a narrow footbridge spanning the stream. I climb down the bank to investigate. It's a bridge all right but only just – a mere strip of concrete with a wire handrail leading nowhere as far as I can see. No sign of a track on the far bank, just a solid mass of heather covering the steep slope. There must have been a purpose for it once but what now?

Upstream the river comes surging over rocky barriers, the water beer-bottle brown as it sweeps over rocks and slides under my feet in a dark surge. A shrubby alder rooted in a rocky islet perkily defies the current. Downstream the river drops noisily out of sight into a winding gorge.

I follow it downstream, negotiating hummocks of moss of the red and green sort (what species I cannot tell), plunging through heather thigh high – waist high, even – stooping under dangling birch and pine branches, following faint animal tracks and water runnels and dodging half-hidden pools brimming with oozy aquatic plant life. Now the river dashes over a rock shelf in a solid chute into a gorge 20 feet below where it boils between high rock walls before emerging, a spent force, in a lazy pool where whorls of foam bubbles sparkle in the sunshine like Milky Ways.

A butterfly settles, brownish with orange roundels on the wings. No doubt Catherine will identify it when I phone.

'Scotch Argus,' she says. 'Common.'

I should have known.

62

Thirty dead alder trees in a line, by my rough count, lean over a stretch of the Cannich River. Naked, stick-like, forked, spiky, mostly stripped of bark and gleaming silvery in the sunlight. Alder, thou art sick; what ails thee?

Frank at Culligran has an answer. He shows a page in a scientific journal headed 'Foliage loss in alders'. Apparently it's widespread. Ten per cent of alder trees in England and Wales have been killed (literally decimated) by the most likely culprit, a fungal disease now ominously spreading northwards. The fungus penetrates the root and works its way up the stem. Symptoms are black tarry patches on the trunk and ill-formed foliage turning yellow and dropping early to leave the crown bare. A nasty ailment with an ugly name – *Phytophthora*.

Surgery does no good. It won't help to chop down a sick tree since the spores, swept along by the current, proceed to attack healthy trees further down river.

Frank says some of his trees at Culligran have been infected. And Tim at Struy says he's noticed a couple of alders on his ground suspiciously thin in the crown. It's scary.

63

Just before the hump bridge at Struy a green-bladed signpost, slightly awry, points the way to Glen Strathfarrar. It's easy to miss. A last-minute swerve may be required.

Half a mile into the glen a gate across the road bars the way. 'Glen closed' it says. How can you close a glen?

A note attached to the gatehouse doorway explains. Cars may not enter on Tuesdays (this is Tuesday) and Wednesday mornings in the season and they're strictly limited in number to 25 at one time. Out of season, never. You may walk in or bike if you like.

Years ago, I first came on this glen and was stopped at the gate. Out from the gatehouse came a large man who issued me with a ticket and told me somewhat grumpily, I thought, to be back by six or I'd be shut in. I read the instructions on the ticket:

> Do not light fires, stoves or other appliances
> Keep dogs on a lead and avoid disturbance of wildlife
> Refrain from moving any plants or animals
> Park with regard for others and take your litter home
> Comply with any request from the warden, the proprietors or their agents, who will identify themselves to you

Five commandments, annotated so:

> These conditions are necessary to protect the beauty of the glen and the scientific interest of the nature reserve. [It's no longer a nature reserve.] Note that no shooting, fishing or camping is allowed. Please drive with care. Maximum speed 30 mph.

I remember that day – the drenching rain, the sight of galleries of tall trees on the far bank of the river and no way to cross to them as the ford marked on the map looked dubious in the extreme.

I love these grand Caledonian pines, seemingly untouched by the ages. That day, I climbed through clumps of old pine trees clustered on either side of a heathery gully through which a burn called the Liatrie romps over a stony bed, crashing over falls in its downward race. The trees were fenced around to keep out deer which would eat the young shoots – protected so that a new flourish of young trees might succeed the old when they die. A cloud of small moths rose at my feet.

On my way back, I saw briars in bloom by the wayside, pink and white. By the waters of Loch Beannacharain, dark and mysterious, a solitary walker down from the misty tops was striding homeward in gaiters and waterproofs sopping wet. I offered him a lift but he preferred independence and marched on. I'd have appreciated his talk, dripping though he was.

My bed for the night was in the youth hostel at Cannich, now closed. It was crowded with a heterogeneous lot, mainly foreigners, Germans, French, Dutch, clashing pans in the kitchen. An Englishman and a couple of grizzled Scots were comparing notes on their hill-climbing day so I escaped for a pint at the then flourishing Glen Affric Hotel across the road. On my return, the trio were still engaged in hill talk.

They asked where I'd been that day. Glen Strathfarrar? Had I done the four? The four? Four what? Then I twigged – they were talking about Munros. Well, I admitted, I wasn't there to climb hills – I was looking at trees. That seemed to perplex them.

Some months later I read the following in *The Coniston Tigers*, a book by the Lakeland writer and climber Harry Griffin (whom I once met at his home in Kendal when he was old): 'One poor day I went off on my own to collect the four Munros in Strath Farrar. After completing the traverse in heavy rain, when swollen burns had to be waded . . .' and so on. When he came down to the road, a man in a car, 'an unusual sight in that glen', offered him a lift which he declined because his gear was so wet.

Cars are no longer unusual in Glen Strathfarrar but they're accepted only on sufferance. Who's glen is it, anyway?

That I may discover.

64

White water explodes in the air, gushing in a halo of iridescence from the base of a little dam. Windborne spray pecks my face. Surrounded by hills of breath-taking grandeur, this miniature dam and its associated works are unspeakably ugly – grey concrete wall, grey windowless cube of a building, grey pipelines reaching up the hillsides on either side like the wings of an anorexic angel. Further upstream, there's another even smaller dam fed by a staircase of many little waterfalls.

Two Land Rovers have halted a little further up the glen. The driver of the foremost, a stalker in tweeds, has stopped to scan the hills through his telescope. His three passengers stare at me blankly as I speak.

'Where are you shooting?'

The stalker points to the hill ahead, Meallan Odhar. Asks, 'Where are you walking?'

'Sgurr na Lapaich.'

'Which way?'

'By the corrie.'

'Fine.'

That concludes the conversation. I shan't disturb their sport. It's been a taciturn exchange between stalker and walker, civil if not affable – not untypical.

This day I hope to climb the Sgurr, the great pyramid at the head of Glen Strathfarrar. Its towering presence has long dominated my thoughts, just as it dominates the upper reaches of the glen.

Steady walking on a good track brings me to the great high corrie under the great rampart of the hill, a waste of broken ground, trackless, cleft by a web of channels and peaty haggs. The last bastion of the hill looms in deep shadow backlit by the descending sun. The waters of two small lochans gleam under it.

As I breast the rim of the corrie, I'm startled by the noise of many voices. Today, at the height of the rut, the corrie is full of echoes as many stags give vent to their lust in testosterone-fuelled bedlam. Rare gulfs of silence are followed by new crescendos.

I'm uneasy, to say the least. Stags are large beasts and, in the rutting season, can be aggressive. Where are they? They're unseen though my ears tell me that they're all around. Sounds come from all quarters. I catch sight of a string of deer moving slowly along a distant ridge, hardly bigger to the naked eye than insects, too far away to count. The roaring ones are well camouflaged in the shadows, present in numbers but not visible to my eye, even with binoculars.

I feel uneasy, menaced. I loiter, lose heart. Do I really want to go on? I convince myself it's late in the day, it's a good hour still to the top, I won't be down before sunset – no. And then, half ashamed of my cowardice, I turn tail.

As I descend by high zigzags, the hills to the north glow in the late sunshine like old friends. I see the bleached shoreline of blue Loch Monar and the glinting thread of the Farrar River gliding sinuously down the glen into the distance. There's a muffled gunshot and then another and, shortly afterwards, I see a couple of figures disappearing round the shoulder of Meallan Odhar – no doubt they're part of the shooting party encountered earlier.

I leave the track to get closer to the burn (the Allt an Eas Bhain Mhoir, a large name for small waters) as it tumbles down by fits and starts, rattling along half-hidden between its banks before plunging abruptly into a narrow gorge. Above the gorge stands a tall aspen tree, the delicate tracery of its thinning autumn leaves illuminated by the sun. In a fortnight's time, it'll be bare. A hoard of small leaves bright as gold coins spilled on the ground lies at my feet.

As I descend I see the stalker's vehicle inching its way along the surfaced track. It crosses ahead of me before I reach the valley bottom and I catch sight of antler tines in the back as it passes – the day's kill.

At the upper dam, the lively burn loses itself, sinking underground in a man-made diversion and echoing from various grilles as it rushes along subterranean channels, leaving the river bed a rubble of dry boulders moistened here and there by a few still pools glazed in a petroly sheen by chemicals in the peat.

The saddest part is to come. I walk across the heath towards a gorge overhung by two small pine trees. I can imagine it as a beauty spot, once. Now it's dry. I walk dryshod over rocks and stones marbled grey and red that once formed the bed of a living river.

But there's to be a resurrection. The spume of water bursting from the mini-dam where I left the car returns the river to its natural course, which now, after its brief hiatus, resumes its course for eventual confluence with the Farrar. Here it's known as the Uisge Misgeach, the drunken water, which is ironic in the present circumstances – it was named long before the hydro engineers tamed it and channelled it underground.

65

On an impulse, I call on Tim, who's just back from the Porsche rally. He pushes aside the laptop and makes coffee. From the window, there's a view of meadows, trees, bare hill and sky. 'I love waking up to the view,' he says.

He and Alice nearly didn't make it to the rally. The Porsche broke down, belching black smoke on its way to a pre-rally service at Oxford. There, the mechanic worked all night rebuilding the engine to get it on the road. It stuttered again in France but was coaxed to Le Mans.

On the way back, still in France, it came to a halt again. Along comes a convoy of fellow rallyists heading for the ferry and, in no time, 30 vintage Porsches are lined up at the side of the road and a scrum of car enthusiasts swarm round the stricken car, heads under the bonnet.

Where's the Porsche now? (There's a gap in the space at the side of the house.)

It's back in Oxford with the man.

66

Frank Spencer-Nairn's home at Culligran is a long white house with a line of attic windows in the roof. It's reached by a lane bordered by alder trees near the bottom of Glen Strathfarrar. A small burn runs alongside, issuing into the wide River Farrar at shingle beds close to the lane end.

Frank's grandfather bought Culligran's several thousand acres of hill and forest from Lovat lands in the 1930s with money made from linoleum. Nairn linoleum was a byword for generations – in the days before fitted carpets it floored countless bourgeois villas and tenement single-ends.

Catherine and I sit in Frank's kitchen (tiled floor, no lino) round a big plain table. There's an Aga, of course, a wine bottle or two on the worktops, picture postcards on the wall. A young German pointer greets us energetically before curling up in his cage in the corner.

There are deer on Frank's hills and salmon and trout in his river – five miles of fishing on his stretch of the Farrar. He lets out the shooting and fishing and, on the odd occasion, he'll go out stalking himself. These are the traditional pursuits of a Highland estate. But Frank has moved with the times. In the 1980s, he diversified into holiday homes – a cottage and five chalets – and, at the same time, he began to farm deer with a nucleus of 60 hinds rounded up in the wild. Now his herd numbers 170 hinds and 11 stags. This month (September), he tells us his shed is full of weaned calves. They'll be despatched to Yorkshire in December to be fattened and killed and the venison will be packaged for the shops.

Frank is the only laird resident in the glen. Five landowners share ownership of long Glen Strathfarrar but only Frank has made his home here. They all visit, of course, and may be seen in the stag-shooting season with guns in their hands or a rod.

He lists them. Frank's cousin Angus, who is something in the City and lives in Jersey, has the Struy Estate on the other side of the river – his son and his family live in Struy Lodge. The Edinburgh lawyer Colin Stroyan has Pait and West Monar at the head of the glen and East Monar is owned by the wealthy David Allen who has featured in the *Sunday Times Rich List*. Finally, there is the mysterious Mr Salleh, Frank's neighbour at Braulen, the largest estate in the glen – a brooding expanse of bare mountain and brown moorland, 30,000 acres of thin soil, rock and heather. Braulen is a Highland sporting estate of the middling kind – good for deer stalking and not much else, economically speaking.

Mr Salleh – if that is his given name (there is uncertainty about it) – is seldom seen. He visits only occasionally. He is said to be a Malaysian of Indian stock. Andy Wightman, writer of the book *Who Owns Scotland*, could discover only that Braulen was acquired in 1990 by a company of Malaysian origin registered in the Cayman Islands and owned by nominee trusts in the Channel Islands.

Frank says he has met Mr Salleh only once in 11 years. Colin Stroyan twice sent word to invite him to dinner and got no response. Sir John Lister-Kaye, the naturalist and author who runs the Aigas field centre, has tried and failed to make his acquaintance.

What can be said of this man of mystery? Scott, who lives in the glen and briefly worked as a gillie at Braulen, remembers him setting out on his first stalk dressed in blue denims with a gold chain round his neck. 'You'd have seen him a mile off.' And so would the stags. Maybe someone had a word with him because, next time, he turned up in tweeds. Iain Mackay, once Iain Thomson's neighbour at the head of Loch Monar, has been a stand-in stalker at Braulen and says he's a good shot. He found him pleasant to work for. 'He won't agree to see anyone but, if you happen to meet him, he's fine.'

George (of Upper Glassburn), when he had the Cnoc Hotel, served Mr Salleh a late dinner when he was on his way to Braulen from the airport. 'He liked the stew,' says George.

And that's as much as I can tell.

Three miles further up the glen from the rock pillar at Loch Beannacharain, Braulen Lodge stands just off the road, a three-gabled, two-storey house of red sandstone. It looks in good trim. In former times before a cash-strapped Lord Lovat sold Braulen, the lodge was smaller, a bit down at heel, though a place of lively social gatherings when the Lovats had shooting guests.

Salleh spruced it up, replaced an unsightly timber annex with a third gable so seamlessly that it's hard to spot the join. Maybe the pink stone of the addition is a little brighter than the time-touched masonry of the original but the change is subtle.

George says stones were dug from the river bed and cut by hand to match the stonework of the house. A squad of specialist masons brought from Glasgow (he thinks they'd been working on Glasgow Cathedral) were so tormented by midges that work had to be halted till the summer was over.

Today, there's no sign of life behind the white metal grille (which has a faintly oriental look) at the front porch, hinting at tight security. I don't ring the bell.

67

It's been raining hard for days. The puddle under the kitchen window (we have taken a week in one of Frank's chalets) grows and grows but today it's dry at last and we take a walk. There's dew on the ground and a touch of frost and the sound of water running through the woods where the river runs fast. Early sunshine falls on leafless trees spotted with lichens and moss.

An electric hum – so we're nearing the power station, a stone-arched cavern in the hillside. A Gaelic inscription: *Neart nan Gleann*, 'Power from the Glens'.

Now there's a rumbling of rushing water. Catherine and I turn into the birch wood to investigate, following an earth track through heather clumps and decayed bracken, wet boggy hollows and outcropping rock. Reaching an abrupt high edge, we see the river below churning through a narrow gorge. Black water swirls between fantastically twisted rock strata. Huge geological pressures formed this cauldron. The map names it Culligran Falls but I guess not many passing strangers find it. Unfrequented except by fishermen, I suspect.

During the morning, snow flurries alternate with spells of sunshine and white clouds moving fast across blue skies. From time to time, the hills are blotted out by storms.

Where the strath opens up into grassy flats and the broad Loch Beannacharain, we reach the rock pillar that indicates the start of Braulen, the neighbouring estate to Culligran. Stags, bearing only the shabby remnants of antlers ready to drop, have come down from the hills for the fodder dumped for them here and twice we see feral goats on the slopes.

It's been a day of all weathers – sun, snow and wind – and, after a bath, our faces glow.

Still it rains. The puddle in the grass below the kitchen window is a miniature loch. It was dry ground when we came.

According to a leaflet left in the chalet, Winans the American magnate and mass slaughterer of deer corralled his stags on the flat ground further up the glen between Loch Beannacharain and Loch a' Mhuilidh. The leaflet contains a veiled warning to wanderers in these parts: 'Hillwalking disturbs the deer and causes extreme inconvenience during the stalking season' and so 'from early September until October 21 permission is likely to be refused'. Signs posted along the glen by the South Ross Deer Management Group are less intimidating: 'The estates in this group recognise the tradition of open access to the hill' – so long as you don't frighten the deer, especially the stags. So keep to the paths. Stags are cash.

This is March. You don't shoot stags in March and we may walk.

In the late afternoon, Catherine and I drive to the head of Glen Strathfarrar and the Monar Dam. The glen grows bleaker by the mile as the mountains close in dark and forbidding. There's snow on the tops, it's sunless and a chill wind blows – a 'thin' wind, you might say.

The road winds on into this remoteness, rising over steep drops until finally it curves round a hillside where a way has been blasted from the bedrock. Old pines cluster in the bottom of the gorge where a meagre river, starved by the half-moon dam, meanders among dry boulders and slabs, running deep only where the channel narrows. A fallen tree, bare and long since dead, lies athwart the riverbed.

We leave the car and walk up the private road towards Monar Lodge and associated buildings, which lie in a dip by the lochside – a timber house, a stone cottage and green-painted sheds. Now Donnie appears, a young man with a round cheery face and stubbly beard under a woolly hat. He tells us he's from Port Glasgow and came here to work as gillie and under-stalker. He'd seen a television programme about a Highland gamekeeper and thought: 'That's the life.' So he quit industrial Clydeside and, nine years later, he's happy here. He likes the lonely life (but admits that he walks his dog less on the open hill now that TV has come to the glen and he watches Sky).

From where we stand, only the eastern end of the loch is visible. Huge mountains surround Loch Monar and these steep monochrome hills of bare rock and heather look fiercely inhospitable on this day – a stark black and white. Shepherding must be difficult in these conditions. What sort of life can it be? It's not for me, no thanks, but Iain Thomson, the isolation shepherd, loved it in his time and so does Donnie now.

68

A hundred bright eyes glint in the gloom of a windowless shed like stars in the night sky. Nervous deer calves huddle in a corner, heads turned towards the light of the opened door. Long-nosed aristocratic faces, pricked ears.

Today their numbers will be swelled from the herd of farmed deer at Culligran, which at present are scattered over an enclosed stretch of tree-studded hillside. The herding party is Frank Spencer-Nairn, big Hamish, who's his manager, Frank's son Douglas and a helper called Julian. I'm on the sidelines, a watcher.

'Our chief management tool is a bag of feed,' says Frank, tipping out a trail of pellets. A string of animals moves closer, warily. Suddenly there's a breakaway and hinds and calves turn tail and flee. Much running and shouting and waving to get them back. Separating calves from their mothers is tricky as they keep dashing for freedom.

When all are rounded up again, the calves are manhandled into pens to be labelled by sex – blue for a male, yellow for a female – which Hamish determines by lifting their tails. Tags are punched into an ear and then a metal disc bearing the animal's number, a statutory requirement. Deer are vulnerable to foot-and-mouth disease and their movements must be recorded. Last thing is to thrust a needle into the rump, which delivers a shot of vitamins, and another under the skin at the shoulder to inject prophylactic drugs.

The calves don't take it calmly. Wide-eyed, they buck and kick, banging against the planks. Sometimes Hamish has to wrestle a lively beast in a headlock. When the last group has gone through the pen, they're marshalled into trailers and taken to the shed to join the others. Their eventual fate – venison cuts on a Waitrose slab.

I talk to Julian. Lean-faced with black hair, nearing 50 I guess, he tells me he was cattleman at nearby Erchless (where years ago Iain Thomson was cattleman for a previous owner) until the boss decided to sell the herd and laid Julian off. A cattleman is a specialist but Julian has had to pick up casual work where he can find it. For the time being, he still lives in a house on the estate and he doesn't want to move – as he says, it's his home and he's among the people he knows.

Weeks later, I pass roadworks near Struy. Among the yellow-jacketed gang is Julian. He waves. Now a road mender.

69

I sit at a table in the window of a café called the Corner on the Square watching the world go by – the world of Beauly, that is. The sun shines and there are people about.

At first sight, the town seems hardly more than a broad square flanked by trim houses and nice shops. Nevertheless, it has a certain charm and status and the Corner, a café-cum-delicatessen selling wines, cheeses and high-class groceries, is a Mecca for ladies of the county set.

The Square's a microcosm. There's a butcher – 'black pudding and haggis champion of the north of Scotland' – a baker and a fruit-and-veg shop – all you need for survival. The Co-op and another small supermarket eye each other from opposite sides of the street. A café humbler than the Corner offers plain fair – coffee, tea, baked potatoes, bacon rolls, egg and chips – plus postcards and assorted tourist ephemera and, this being the sunny side of the square, two tables are set out on the pavement – Beauly caff goes continental. There's a hotel, the Priory, with attached rhyming (and punning) fish and chip shop, 'the Friary', a gift shop, an art shop with paintings in large gilt frames, the accent being on sheep and gloomy heather moors, and a pub. Maggie Blyth – there *is* a Maggie Blyth, I have met her – is a chic dress shop for sophisticated ladies. Here, Catherine has shopped and I have bought for her. Hard by, for a time, was Maggie Blyth Men, a similar showcase for stylish males, where sitting at his desk was

Garry Blyth himself, coiffed, with a cravat at his neck. Alas, Maggie Blyth Men did not last. On a return visit, I find it shuttered and bare.

In the centre of the Square, a small stone obelisk commemorates war dead – not those of the world wars but men who died in South Africa in the Boer War of 1899–1902. There's a particular reason for this. The inscription tells that it was erected in 1905 by Lovat tenantry to commemorate the raising of the Lovat Scouts for service in South Africa by Simon Joseph 16th Lord Lovat 'who desired to shew that the martial spirit of their forefathers still animates the Highlanders of to-day and whose confidence was justified by the success in the field of the gallant corps whose existence was due to his loyalty and patriotism'. It was Lovat's belief that stalkers and gillies, marksmen all, handy with their ponies and trained in stealthy approach over rough country, would be well qualified to meet the Boer irregulars on the veldt. Many enlisted.

All Strathglass was Lovat country. Their lands stretched from Beauly to the far west and the Lovat baronial seat, Beaufort Castle, is just a mile or two away – former seat, it should be said, for, now that the Lovat wealth and lands have been frittered away, it belongs to Ann Gloag of Stagecoach, businesswoman and philanthropist. Close to the Square is a house that used to be the Lovat Estate office and, beside that, the Lovat Arms Hotel, grandest building in town – *modestly* grand, as befits the place – somewhat French in style with mansard roof. Here Catherine and I spent a couple of nights, attracted by its homely atmosphere – log fire blazing in the hearth – and sleeping under a canopy swagged in tartan. One night, a party of elderly bus trippers made merry in the dining room. One dame in her 70s introduced us to her companion: 'He's not my husband – he's the boyfriend.' Cackle, cackle.

A short step from the Square, there is a time capsule: Campbell and Co., Highland outfitters 'by royal appointment' (the Queen Mum), where you may be served by the latest Campbell in the line and his two elegant sisters. Here I place an order for breeks or plus-twos, the tweed breeches worn as working garb by stalkers and farmers and casually by the gentry and wealthy visitors who like to show a well-turned leg.

In a small back room lined with pictures of tartan-clad clansmen, silver-haired James Campbell takes my measurements, shows his pattern books and I choose a check. It's a surprise to see how many colours are combined in the weave though the overall effect is muted – there are at least three shades of green, from olive to very nearly black, through which run thin lines of mustard and red.

James lays out his two big pattern books on the table – *Scottish Estate Tweeds* and *Our Scottish District Checks* – heavy, floppy volumes of sample patches. In the old days, lairds used to dress their servants with their own choice of livery. Estate tweeds were big business when small armies of outdoor workers were employed – keepers, stalkers, gillies, gardeners, foresters and hands, all to be clad. It's still done, though on a lesser scale, says James. When an estate changes hands it's not unusual for the new owner, English, American, Scandinavian or Arab perhaps, to change the livery to a style more to his taste.

He's heard tales of his grandfather taking to the moors in company with a landed client to match the colours of a proposed tweed to the tones of the heather, the grasses, the mosses. In what season? For the colours change. Late summer and early autumn might be best when the sporting season is at its height.

You step inside the shop and feel the years roll back – wooden shelves heaped with rolls of tweed, deerstalker hats, pork pies and other country headgear piled up in pagoda-like stacks, racks of heavyweight jackets and breeches – such an air of yesteryear. An American who came into the shop was so entranced that he photographed it from every angle, saying that he wanted to replicate it in the States.

But what's to come? Some day, all this must change and probably not for the better. Ian at Comar Lodge thinks so. He forecasts that the Campbells will eventually sell and whoever buys the shop won't keep it that way and may not even continue the business. It's the prime site on the main street and it's not the tweeds sold there that counts. The ironmonger's next door was similarly old-fashioned until it was reinvented 20 years ago – although not wholly, for the wooden stairs creak as they always did and there's still old timber panelling on the upper floor.

James Campbell would hate the shop to change but there's no one to take over – he and his sisters are the last of the line. They'll have no trouble selling. When they moved from the flat above the shop to a bungalow nearby, rumours circulated that they were giving up the business and offers to buy flooded in.

The business began in 1858 under a different name and the Campbell interest came when James's grandfather married a daughter of the firm. It's been Campbell & Co. since the 1920s. James says the '70s to the '90s were the boom years, with the bulk of the trade coming from American visitors. Now there are fewer Americans around and business is calmer.

Royalty has shopped here, hence the coat of arms on the facade. The Queen Mother would despatch an equerry for her shopping and Princess Margaret came in person. Camilla has been but not Charles so far. The coat of arms – 'by royal appointment' – has to come down under a rule that declares it must be removed five years after the royal customer's death. It will then join another in the attic from the short reign of Edward VIII. Did Mrs Simpson ever call? Probably not.

James is no ordinary tailor and outfitter. He's been made a papal knight, at the mention of which he smiles deprecatingly. How many of us have had their inside leg measured by a papal knight?

70

In a small antique shop just off the Square, the lights glint on silver and a shelf crowded with Staffordshire figures, historic and mythical, including the Gladstones, Mr and Mrs. He's severe, she frumpish. Who'd buy Mr Gladstone now, four times prime minister, classical scholar and grand old man though he was in his time? I for one, if I'd the money to spare – I've a soft spot for him.

There's local interest. Gladstone came to Guisachan as a house guest when elderly and out of office and past all thought of wielding his axe on Tweedmouth trees.

The Staffordshire Gladstone is ghostly in plain white glaze relieved only by a hint of gold on the waistcoat, a touch of black on his toecaps and black pinpoint eyes. I could have had him for £145 or £400 the pair. So he's worth more with his missus than alone.

71

Strolling in the Square in the evening, I stop at the art shop to gaze at a large coloured engraving on an easel in the window. It's a stalking scene – or, rather, an *après* stalking scene. In the foreground, figures in Highland dress led by a piper cross a humpback bridge. There's a gillie with the dogs and, on the crown of the bridge, the chieftain walks tall, a tartan plaid slung over his shoulder and a feather in his cap, followed by two retainers and a boy leading two ponies with stags slung sack-like across their backs, antlers spiked against the sky. In the rear, a stalker with guns on his shoulder chats to a group of peasant women at the wayside. A sliver of blue loch is just visible beyond, with snow-capped hills in the distance. A copperplate inscription reads *The Chief's Return from Deer Stalking* and the artist is named as Sir Edwin Landseer.

Landseer, a great favourite of the Victorians, is unfashionable now but this Landseer I liked. It's deer stalking as grand opera. Did it ever happen that way? Since Landseer took pride in the accuracy of his scenes despite a tendency to romanticise, it probably did. It's different nowadays. Where's your Highland dress, the full panoply? And the ponies? Gone, mostly, ousted by the stalkers' Argocats and Land Rovers.

Next morning, I return to the shop and a deal is done. *Return from Stalking* is lifted from its easel and put into store to be collected later and I amble back to the guest house where I've spent the night.

This guest house is rather grand in its way – a large villa close to the Square with spacious rooms reached by a handsome staircase. On the landing stands a wardrobe in dark figured wood garnished with carved oak leaves, about nine feet tall and wide in proportion. Thinking of *The Lion, the Witch and the Wardrobe*, I sneak a glance inside but it doesn't lead to Narnia. The way is blocked by neat piles of bed linen.

72

A gate leads off the Square into the grounds of a ruined priory as reclusive as the monks who once lived there – a gaunt building screened by big trees. Grandest of all is a sycamore with a huge spread of foliage held aloft on up-stretched boughs. But the elm tree beside the gate is a sad spectacle – an ancient ruin to match the priory. It's said to have been planted by Mary Queen of Scots and looks its age – a time-wizened stem leaning at an angle, shorn of its crown from which a cluster of sprouting shoots indicate the last snatch at life of a decaying leviathan. Two more elderly elms shade the few gravestones at their feet. One, split down the middle and held together by webbing straps, gets regular health checks and medication from Historic Scotland.

First glimpse of the building is of a bare red sandstone gable where the great window was, stark against the sky. The body of the church is roofless. The nave is high and narrow, with tombstones sunk flat on the turf floor. On one side are three pear-shaped windows, the stone salt-bitten and etched by wind and rain. There's a feeling of arrested decay about the place. Why was it abandoned to the elements and when? Possibly misguided zealotry on the part of Protestant reformers, the dilapidating rage of religious fundamentalists. The glib answer is to blame John Knox.

According to an information panel, the priory was established in 1230 though the ruined building dates from later. It was, it says on the board, a Valliscaulian foundation – an order of monks which took its name from its place of origin, the Val-des-Choux (Valley of the Cabbages) near Dijon. A maximum of 20 monks was permitted in Valliscaulian houses and it's suggested that Beauly housed no more than a handful. Only the prior had contact with the world.

Life was hard. Silence reigned. They had no mattresses. A thankless regime. They lived in hope of what? Of their daily bread and ale or of something more than the bare necessities? Salvation, I guess.

73

The station at Beauly is really only a halt. You stick your hand out and the train stops. A single line of rail curls round the tiny platform which is only one coach long. Beauly scrapes on to the railway map but only just.

To the left, the line disappears under the road through an arch of red sandstone, buttressed these days by concrete. That way leads, several hours up the line, to Thurso and Wick in the far north. Inverness is the other way. At the end of the short platform, signs poke out from spires of rosebay willow herb warning: 'Do not alight here'. You'd tumble into the undergrowth if you did. '

'Alight' – it's curious word, gives pause for thought. Railways like it but you don't see it much elsewhere. I look up a dictionary. '*Rather formal or old use*,' says Chambers. '*Poetic*,' says another. Or, as Samuel Johnson had it long ago, 'The word implies the idea of descending; as, of a bird from the wing, a traveller from his horse or carriage.'

On this sunny morning, delicate leaves of wych elm flutter down from the trees to settle on the track. Oddments of debris litter the elderly wooden sleepers – an old glass bottle, once green but now opaque, coated with black oil as if transmuted. When did I last see timber sleepers? Ageing, dark brown, knotted and split – a reminder of the time when wheels on rails went clickety-click and still do here.

A peacock butterfly settles on the platform edge, unfolding its wings to the sun's rays. 'A peacock alighted (alit?) on the platform edge' – *poetic*.

74

In bed at Comar Lodge, reaching for a book to read from the selection on the bedside table, I find this: *Paul Kruger, His Life and Times*, a faded edition of more than 30 years ago by a Cambridge academic. Boer Wars etc. – a bit esoteric for a B&B. I wonder who left it there.

I read Kruger's words, I hear them gruff and guttural: 'Whether we conquer or die, freedom will come to Africa as surely as the sun rises through tomorrow's clouds . . . Then shall it be from Zambesi to Simon's Bay, Africa for the Afrikanders.' Wrong, of course – when freedom came, the sun rose not on Afrikaaners but black Africans.

75

Scott multi-tasks. He grows his own food. He drives a van for the library service, delivering books to the housebound. He takes a hand with the desktop publishing business his wife runs – she's also the school secretary. And he's the district's part-time registrar.

Deanie is two houses and a ruin reached by way of a rough track. It's the last outpost of Lovat land in the glen, sandwiched as it is between Mr Salleh's Braulen Estate and Frank Spencer-Nairn's Culligran.

We sit on a bench looking down the garden Scott made – a tiny pool, poppies in bloom, other flowers and shrubs and a vegetable patch, of course. He points to the corner where he has planted the Gaelic alphabet – in other words, the 18 trees which, in folklore, represent the Gaelic letters. They're growing sturdily – Gaelic thrives in his garden. He says that, when he came to Deanie, it took three days to move in all his household goods mainly because of the compost, which is close to his heart. He loaded it onto a trailer and brought it all with him. 'I couldn't leave it,' he says, feelingly.

Being a peripatetic registrar here can be demanding. One wedding at which he officiated took place beside a lochan above Loch Monar, a romantic spot or so the happy couple thought until the tempest struck. The wind howled and the rain bucketed. A dozen or so guests including a mother and her seven-month-old baby turned up for the ceremony, dripping, some trudging up the muddy track, others jolting along in a stalkers' vehicle. They'd brought a tent but failed to pitch it in the storm so the wedding took place in the open and, on the way down, the walkers had to wade through two burns in spate.

76

It's 10 miles round Loch Affric. The river's in turmoil and all the burns are high, spilling over the rough track often ankle deep. I splash through on submerged stone, thinking, 'What will these burns be like later when the sodden hills have released all their weight of water?' Stalkers' vehicles have churned the peat in many places and, a short way off the track, I see two figures hunched in a parked Argocat, peering into the gloom. Not a good day for their sport, I guess.

Out of the landscape comes the only human I'll meet from first to last, a young Frenchman, heavily laden, who's trekked in from the west coast, having stopped overnight at Alltbeithe. It's not the weather that bothers him, he says, but the midges.

In Cannich, I dry off in the Slaters Arms and, coming out, I meet John MacLennan, his face burnished by the wind. He's been out on the hill all day.

'Have a dram,' I say.

But he declines. 'I've had a few already,' he responds with that wee smile of his.

77

The turbines are running at Fasnakyle Power Station – I know because of the Niagara cascading into the river below it, churning the stream into whirlpools. The power station, dominating a bend in the Affric, is a handsome building in blond stone which I admire every time I pass. There's even sculpture on the facade – Celtic beasts carved by Hew Lorimer, a sculptor who, like his mentor Eric Gill, believed that art has a spiritual function. Let there be light and there was light – with the help of the North of Scotland Hydroelectric Board.

A man in a yellow hard hat doesn't think I should enter but I manage to glance through the open door of the turbine hall. It's high, bright and airy, with three turbine domes in line down the centre of the floor like giant toadstools. There's a sudden blast of colour – blue turbines, white walls, green steel girders high up under the yellow roof supporting a yellow travelling crane.

What a space. It takes the breath away. Why, it could even become the Highland Tate Modern, some day. Smaller than that London one, true, but brighter.

78

A horse has been seen inside the old Glen Affric Hotel.

Inside? That's right. At a window looking out. Two people have told me so.

I know Louise has a horse, but this?

I don't know what to think.

79

Walter and Bob bustle into the kitchen at the Backpackers. Walter is tall and long-legged, a bit gaunt, with white wavy hair. Bob is bald, maybe a bit shorter, plumper and he wears glasses. They've just arrived after tramping up several hills together and tomorrow they'll climb some more. Walter and Bob are seasoned in the hills.

We share the last couple of inches in Walter's whisky bottle and, when that's done, Bob uncorks another. *Slainte!* They invite me to share their meal of beans and bolognaise and potatoes all mixed up in the same pot.

This pair could reminisce about hills all night long. Mam Sodhail isn't difficult, says Walter, big hill though it is. There's a good path right to the top. He says there's a big cairn and the ruin of a stone hut at the summit.

After supper, they head for a pint at the Slaters Arms while I stay on to write up notes. My cell-like room is bare and somewhat chilly. A smell of stale smoke from last night's fire drifts from the stove in the lounge. It's not cosy.

So I phone George at Upper Glassburn and book a room for tomorrow night. 'Would you have dinner?' No need to ask.

80

The old Scottish Mountaineering Club's well-thumbed guide *The Western Highlands*, published nearly 80 years ago, may not be up to date but, between its faded red covers, it still makes good reading. I can't say the same for the maps. The scale is too small, the detail too crowded and the emphasis whimsical. Beauly is set in bigger type than Inverness, which can never have seemed right. Drumnadrochit rates notice only as Drumnadrochit Hotel and there's no mention of Cannich at all, just the Glen Affric Hotel. Loch Beinn a'Mheadhoin is spelt in the old style, as pronounced – Beneveian – which I can approve of.

This note occurs:

> Mam Sodhail and Sgurr na Lapaich. On account of their commanding position in the North-West of Scotland these two mountains were made important stations for the Principal Triangulation in connection with the Ordnance Survey of the British Isles. The station on Mam Sodhail was on the highest point of the mountain, and was marked by a stone pile, 23 feet high and 60 feet in circumference . . .

That's a lot of stones.

A more recent Munro book tells more: 'The summit has a huge circular cairn which was an important point in the Ordnance Survey's primary triangulation of Scotland in the 1840s.'

In the National Library of Scotland's map room in Edinburgh, I open a large leather-covered volume – *Account of the Observations of the Principal Triangulations*, being an 'account of the Observations of the Principal Triangulation; and of the Figure, dimensions & mean specific gravity of the Earth as derived therefrom', drawn up, as it says, by Captain Alexander Ross Clarke of the Royal Engineers.

I read that among the sites from which observations were made was 'the mountain of Mamsuil [*sic*] on the borders of the counties of Ross and

Inverness, about 7 miles north-west of Captain Inge's shooting lodge at Glen Affaric and 20 miles west of Inverncannich'.

On this summit, a Colour-Sergeant J Winzer and his party of soldier-surveyors lodged or camped throughout the month of August and possibly longer in 1848, scanning the surrounding high points, taking bearings, measuring angles and recording distances. Rain, hail or shine. It can be wild up there in any season but the official report makes no mention of the weather.

I shall follow in your footsteps, Sergeant Winzer.

81

The forecast's not good. North-westerly winds up to 30 miles an hour on the hills 'will impede steady walking on higher exposed areas'. Risk of one or two flurries of hail and snow on the highest summits.

Mam Sodhail is 1,181 metres (3,862 feet old style) – you don't get much higher. But, if not now, when?

I'm on the track along Loch Affric, north side, at 8.20 in the morning. The sky's a welter of varying shades of grey with fast-moving clouds parting and swiftly closing over scant patches of blue. There's some hope but it's dark and sombre over by Kintail where the weather's coming from. The wind whips up waves across the loch and there's a line of thin foam where they break on the shore.

Seen from a distance, the path ascending the deep-cut glaciated valley appears as a long brown thread. The multitudinous burns are knotted strands of white water. Somewhere above is the hill, invisible as yet in a dense bank of mist. Stray shafts of wan sunlight cast pools of bright green on the hillside with theatrical effect. An embryonic rainbow flickers through the mist.

The way, washed by floodwater, is stony and steep. Loose stones clatter and roll under my feet – such attractive stones they are, rounded and veined and glistening in the wet.

I linger in the corrie, hoping for signs that the mist will clear for a decent interval. A sudden glimpse of the summit is all too brief – the veil falls again but there's sufficient promise to draw me onwards. In a grassy meadow under an abrupt scarp, an infant burn exits from a pool, whence the path climbs steeply in measured zigzags up to the ridge. It's a craftwork of canny engineering from Victorian days when stalkers' paths were maintained and it still serves. Here Sergeant Winzer and his companions sweated in their serge uniform jackets in the summer of '48. Here their ponies or mules picked their way up, labouring under loads of timber for building, the heavy theodolite and its associated impedimenta, food and cooking utensils, everything required for their encampment. Was there a regular traffic up and down this track during their occupation of the mountain top or did they hold out, isolated, cut off for the duration? I can only speculate.

Behind me, the glen unfolds below in a long bare corridor reaching towards the loch shore. There's no sign of life on the path though it's visible for most of its length. No other walker has appeared all day. It seems strange to have this hill all to myself when the summer's barely gone.

On the exposed ridge, the wind is less fierce than anticipated, buffeting me and chilling my hands but less troublesome than the forecast implied. It's easy walking now – a low-angled ascent over firm ground littered with stones. A corner of drystane wall emerges from the dimness, the remains of a substantial hut – two chambers linked by a low arch. I have to duck to enter.

The mist clears briefly. Views come and go in swift succession and suddenly the cairn built by the triangulators of '48 appears on the crest – a squat circular wall like an Iron Age broch broken-off at the top. It's solidly built like some kind of fortification (army engineers knew their masonry defences) and about nine feet high, half its original height. When whole, it must have been awesome.

82

In June 1945, just as the war in Europe ended, Duncan MacLennan climbed Mam Sodhail on business. He tells me about it by his fireside in

Cannich – brings out a faded sheet of paper with torn edges, ripped from a jotter by the look of it. On this is written:

> Ordnance Survey copy to D Maclennan, Glen Affric Lodge. To hire of four ponies over rough steep track to top of Mam Soul with cement and sand, rate £1. 1s per day: £4. 4s. With expenses (hauling of cement, sand etc to top of Mam Soul and expenses in connection with same): £19 . . . [illegible]

That June, Duncan spent four days assisting in the construction of a trig pillar for the Ordnance Survey on top of Carn Eighe, Mam Sodhail's twin peak. The laden ponies stopped short of the final dip and ascent, leaving their burden to be manhandled up a last treacherous scree slope.

Duncan says the sand was dug from the shore at the head of Loch Affric and ferried across the loch to a landing stage at the start of the climb. Two of the beasts of burden were his own deer ponies and he hired two more for the job. The six Ordnance Survey men had no easy task – he recalls them lugging heavy car batteries on their shoulders for lighting at the top. They worked non-stop, he says. 'They just didn't have enough hours in the day.'

As for the derelict bothy, he doesn't associate it with the survey party of the 1840s. More likely, he says, it would have been built as a shelter for the guards installed there to spy out deer poachers – a lonely outpost.

83

Notice outside the Tomich Post Office:

> Butterflies of the glen, how to identify and record them, Saturday 27. Strathglass shinty club, next game at Cannich, throw-up 2.30pm. Strathglass community council minutes: report on pylons; proposed alteration to Glen Affric Hotel – application for a bar.

I've heard about this proposed bar. But it's not Louise. Maybe she has a tenant.

84

The October weather's bright with a nip in the air and clear skies morning, noon and night. This is the season to see Affric at its best, when the birch is ablaze with colour.

We have taken Chalet Number 9 in the village of Cannich for a week. We have laid in a store of provisions, with books to read, wines red and white and malt whisky for a dram at night. We have our boots; we shall walk out by day, turn up the heating in the evening and sleep snug under doubled duvets.

At eight in the morning, I'm scraping frost from the windscreen, Catherine still in bed (bad back). By nine o'clock I'm striding along by the lochside. The sun's low, the sky a tent of unbroken blue, the water glassy dark, a perfect mirror for trees and hills.

I climb through close-growing plantation trees dripping with swags of grey lichen, labouring as I cross ridges and ruts made by the foresters who ploughed up the ground before planting. Now the corrugations are mantled with thick spongy moss. It's good to breathe lungfuls of crisp air.

I emerge from the plantation to find steep slopes and heathery bluffs above. Below my feet, the crust of frosty soil is softening as the sun gains strength. The view is spectacular. The long dark loch seen through cohorts of majestic pine trees stretches below me, its outline broken by green promontories and pine-shaggy islands. Far mountains are white with snow.

Peace. A crystal silence, broken only by the faint hoarse baying of a lone lusting stag echoing across the water.

I scramble among heathery ledges, skirting icy patches, until, on the edge of a steep drop among sentinel pines, I get a pulse of excitement – this, surely, is the spot where the photographer Robert Moyes Adam set up his camera almost 80 years ago. The caption on the photograph I clutch in cold fingers reads: 'Loch Beinn a'Mheadhoin with birch and pine forest, Glen Affric, 10 April 1929'. My view matches his exactly. The black-and-white photograph shows a rock-littered slope with trees below and a long boomerang of loch filling the hollow. Scattered pine and birch still flourish as he saw them through the lens but, where the plantation grows, the hillside was bare in his day. A corner of Loch Affric shows as a dot of water in the distance. White-rimmed clouds give hints of pale sunshine.

The rising sun behind me casts long shadows. The gaunt distant hills are touched with a rosy flush. I gaze but not for long. I have to get back. Boots ring pleasantly on the hard surface as I tramp along the forest track. The car's still in deep shade and the lock's frozen, causing some minutes of frustration before I manage to open the door.

I drive down the long glen and reach Cannich just after 11. And, at four in the afternoon, C and I are strolling in T-shirts by the loch, millpond calm with the glory of golden birch among dark pines reflected in the water.

'Not more than two per cent of all my pictures are taken from anywhere near a road,' said Robert Moyes Adam, who roamed throughout Scotland with a half-plate camera recording nature. There's a photograph of him on a pony taken far up Glen Affric. He probably set the camera on its tripod and focussed for a helper to take the shot.

He came to Glen Affric in 1929 and returned a year later, prompted by plans to harness Highland rivers for the generation of electricity. A private company had a bill before parliament which proposed to dam the three great lochs of the Beauly catchment in Glen Affric, Glen Cannich and Glen Strathfarrar in order to generate hydroelectric power on a large scale. Horrified at the prospect, Adam set out with his bulky equipment to record the beauties and hopefully stop the desecration.

I found his sequence of Affric pictures in the photo archive at St Andrews University and have some of the prints with me. Can I find the sites? See what's changed? I shall try.

At the foot of the glen we catch sight of a cyclist flickering through the trees – Tony from Skipton, speeding down the Glen Affric road on his bike in his yellow top and an old check cap on his head. Tony and I first met a month ago in a walkers' hostel in Kintail and got on famously. We thought we might meet again here. He pedals furiously out of sight without seeing us but I call on him at the hostel in Cannich and tonight he'll come to dinner.

We have soup, we have stew, we uncork the bottle. Grey-bearded, ruddy-faced, bright-eyed behind his specs, Tony talks – how he talks! – in a thick Yorkshire accent compounded by his helter-skelter way with words. I could have done with subtitles. He tells long tales of how he'd worked in factories, set up as a window cleaner, lived with his mother and devoted his time to nursing her when she was ill. When she died, he turned his hobby to advantage – always a club cyclist, he got on his bike and rode round the country taking pictures to sell for postcards and calendars.

He's regularly in Affric in October because the autumn fire in the leaves reflected in the water makes for spectacular pictures. A trip covers his costs and he doesn't ask for more. Hostels and bunkhouses provide a bed. He travels light with just two of everything – shirts, pants and vests – and every second day he washes them.

Tony lives alone but says he's never lonely. He cycles with his club every weekend and, this Christmas, they'll all go to Ambleside – to the hostel, of course.

Then he mounts his bike and pedals off into the frosty night. We like Tony but I don't suppose we'll meet again. Maybe some day I'll find his name on a postcard – Picture: Tony Rostron.

Beinn nan Sparra. The photograph shows a bare hilltop with a large tilted rock prominent in the foreground like a sea creature breaking the surface. 'Glen Affric from Beinn nan Sparra with lochs Affric and Beinn a'Mheadhoin, 3 April 1929.' Adam wrote a brief description on the print: 'Grassy slope with rocky outcrops to the fore; rocks and trees on lower slope; lochs and snow-capped peaks on horizon.'

It's almost noon when we set off. We have a key for the padlocked gate allowing us to drive along the south shore of Loch Beinn a'Mheadhoin to a fork in the forest road where we park. Larch and pines – Scots pine and the black-veined Corsican pine – gladden the way. A grassy path beckons into the woods, a glade walk overhung with delicate birch branches. Stony patches indicate that it may have been an old drove road, now overgrown and neglected.

The track peters out among plantation conifers and we come to a clearing of oozy heather bog encircled by thick forest, noticing the white plastic supermarket bag hanging from a branch where we emerge. We splodge across yielding ground but find no gap in the thick barrier of evergreen to continue on our way. It's impenetrable – a hedge for Sleeping Beauty. There's nothing for it but to return to the plastic bag, tied there no doubt as a guide to the lost like us.

Little Loch na Gabhlach, when we discover it behind a light screen of birch trees, is a dream – hardly more than a pond rimmed with reeds, dappled with lily pads and ringed by a circle of dark trees. A bed of golden moss gleams in an inlet beside the bone-white stem of a dead tree and a slender young pine. A flight of small birds skims soundlessly across the surface.

Across from where we stand, a fringe of evergreen trees lit by a glint of watery sunshine casts reflections on the surface, with blue rugged hills rising above. These trees, dense and geometrically ordered, planted possibly 30 years ago, have grown tall and stately. In forestry terms, they're ripe for felling but I hope they'll be reprieved. Let them mature in peace. There's an air of Canadian wilderness about this lochan. A birch bark canoe on its waters wouldn't seem out of place.

A little further on and we come on a second lochan, Loch Carn na Glas-leitre, larger and gloomier than Gabhlach, with a single islet in the centre. Littering the ground around is a brash of young lodgepole pine felled in the name of nature conservation (because they're an 'alien' species – i.e. not Scots pines). Dry bones, sapless, bleached white.

Beinn nan Sparra comes into view – a long rough ridge thinly dotted with pines. A fence bars the way to the top and I clamber over but

Catherine, suffering from her bad back, prefers to sit in the sunshine while I explore further, wandering among dips and knolls in search of the Adam view. It never seems right. The loch cannot be the same, of course, for the shoreline is 20 feet higher than it was in Adam's day and islands and inlets have been swamped. The sea-monster rock is nowhere to be found.

A faint shout carries in the still air and I catch sight of Catherine's blue jacket on a hilltop some distance away. I must have ranged wider than I thought and I make haste to join her, sweating with the exertion.

'Glen Affric with Loch Affric and site of Glen Affric Lodge, looking westward, 8 April 1929.'

Look westward we do. We're at the Steven memorial with the distant blue hills of Kintail in view. A narrow mud path leads up through the trees to this viewpoint or belvedere where there is a tablet inscribed to Professor H. M. Steven and others unnamed who first campaigned for the conservation of the old Caledonian pinewoods. Steven wrote an influential book *The Native Pinewoods of Scotland* with his co-author Jock Carlisle, a young research fellow at Aberdeen University. The prof devised the strategy, Carlisle did the legwork – he walked these hills in rain, sun and snow in search of the ancient woods. I met Jock Carlisle in Canada and I have the book.

Below us, a ribbon of water between the lochs Beinn a'Mheadhoin and Affric reflects the evening sky, calm and pearly. We are near where Adam stood on that April day – perhaps among those pine trees clustered on a knoll about a quarter of a mile away.

We trudge through rank heather and boggy hollows to the knoll, a hogs-back littered with tumbled rocks, among which the old pines grow tall. They're in disarray – some fallen and rotting in the mossy bed, others dead but still standing among a litter of twigs and shed branches.

We clamber over rocks and recumbent tree trunks, ducking under low branches until, at last, checking with the photograph, every feature falls into place – the wooded headland, the cottage on the inlet, the trestle bridge beside it, the bend in the narrow road, the serpentine head of the loch, the water calm and palely glimmering, the far-off hills touched by shafts of sunshine. The pair of tall pine trees that framed his shot still stand. Few time-elapsed changes are apparent – the road is now partly obscured by a later flush of birch but, essentially, the scene is as Adam caught it. This is where he stood – we see with Adam's eyes.

I have one more photograph but there's no time to follow it up – we have to leave for home. I'll be back.

85

May, six months later and I have returned alone. The Adam photo shows pale Loch Affric in the distance backed by rising hills, the tops streaked with snow, prominent among them the elegant spire of Sgurr na Lapaich with a slash of white water on its flank where a burn drops towards the loch. In the middle distance a man in a tweed jacket sits astride a dappled pony, broad-backed and round-bellied, on a narrow track. He holds the reins loosely in his hands. His face is turned towards the camera but, at this distance, the features are indistinct. The track winds through a thick ground cover of heather. In the foreground are three pine trees and a sapling on a mound. 'R M Adam on deer pony, Athnamulloch path, Glen Affric, 18 April 1930.'

The shutter clicked three-quarters of a century ago but the scene, I guess, should be much the same today.

A second shot taken from a different angle shows the pony with another man in the saddle and a figure standing knee-deep in the heather behind him. 'W Finlayson, stalker and resident of Alltbeithe, with postman.'

It's many years since any postman carried the mail this far up the glen. It's also years since Alltbeithe was an inhabited house. There's only a youth hostel at Alltbeithe now, one of the remotest, far out west on the track to Kintail.

Old Duncan, who was a teenage boy when the photos were taken, peers at the print. Even at 90 his memory is keen but the name W Finlayson doesn't ring a bell. 'There was a Henderson at Allbeithe about that time,' he says. 'A Donald Finlayson lived at Camban' – but Donald Finlayson left the glen before Adam's visit. And anyway Camban, a cottage further up the glen and even more isolated than Alltbeithe, has been empty since 1926.

It's unseasonably wet and cold. Flurries of driving rain with a touch of sleet in it, swelling storm clouds chasing glints of sunshine across the sky, the cliff face of Sgurr na Lapaich squall-streaked and edged with snow. At the car park, a party of climbers, booted, gaitered and waterproofed, set off for the hill. I don't envy them. I keep to the low ground on the Athnamulloch path, these days metalled and upgraded to a forestry track.

Keeping an eye open for likely spots, branching off the track in search of a matching view, map blobbed by rain and flapping in the wind... nothing conforms. As I emerge from deep vegetation at the trackside, a tall figure in a squashy yellow oilskin hat is taken by surprise at my sudden appearance. We put our heads together over the photograph. 'You need to be higher,' he says and I agree.

We walk on, chatting, Adam forgotten. The stranger is Dutch. 'My name is Dirk but you can call me Dick.' Dick or Dirk tells me he had a florist's shop near Rotterdam but sold it when his wife died and he turned 60. Now he takes long trips to Scotland every summer. Last year, it was Aviemore – next year, perhaps Orkney. Is it good in Orkney? I say yes – wide horizons, big skies, high cliffs, lots of standing stones.

The white cottage with the red tin roof at Athnamulloch comes into view on grassy flats, where our paths separate. Dirk walks on towards Alltbeithe, I cross a burn by a wobbly plank and peer into the cottage window. There's no sign of life but people have spent time here recently – there's a couple of bottles on the ledge, one whisky and the other sloe gin, an odd coupling, and a scatter of paperbacks, one called *Comanche*. Welcome to the Wild West, Athnamulloch.

I retrace my steps and resume the search. So many trees but never the right ones until, on a whim, I make a rapid descent through 50 yards of rank vegetation and suddenly Adam's three trees are before me just as he pictured them. A branch or two may have fallen or bent further towards the ground but the kink in the spindly third tree (now dead and leafless) is unmistakable. Every distant peak on the horizon matches.

The odd thing is there's no sign of the track which is so clearly seen in the photograph. The meandering pathway where the pony stood with Adam on its back has disappeared – obliterated, as I now realise, by a mantle of heather, moss and coarse grasses. Nature has reclaimed her own. Somewhere under my feet, the old stony surface lies buried, abandoned when the forest road was made on a different line. The old Athnamulloch path has vanished from the face of Affric, along with Adam, stalker Finlayson and the anonymous postman of 80 years ago.

86

Ian, seventh son at Cougie, drives a tractor under the gaze of his two tousle-headed boys. He wears a fur hat skin side out like Davy Crockett's. I ask him where to find what's left of the Iron Fence and he points the way.

I first heard of the Iron Fence years ago when Catherine and I trekked through Glen Affric and found a reference to it at the Alltbeithe hostel – the note on the kitchen wall that told how, late in the 19th century, 'West Affric became part of the massive deer forest of a railway magnate called Winans.'

Donald Fraser's booklet on Guisachan tells more. By the 1870s, bit by bit, the American tycoon Winans had acquired shooting rights over 350 square miles of bleak mountain and moorland stretching from Beauly in the east to Kintail in the west. He had a great fence erected around this vast territory, snaking over hill and hollow in order – so he hoped – to prevent the deer on his land from straying on to neighbouring estates. He considered the deer his own. Small furnaces for the blacksmiths he employed on the work flared along the line in the mountain wilderness.

I set off along a forest road though a great slice of the forest has gone, felled, logged and extracted except for a few naked stems left standing as habitat for birds and burrowing insect. Drifts of pale sawdust surround newly cut stumps alongside the road and the air is heavy with the smell of resin.

I pass into Mr Kwint's West Guisachan estate ('Walkers welcome', it says on the gate, with the usual proviso about the shooting season – in sum, walk on if you like but don't stray from the track) and stop by a lochan which seems much larger than it's shown on my map. Old map – after this edition was made, a small dam was built to enlarge the lochan for fishing, common practice in this fishing country.

I sit on the low curve of masonry that serves as a dam, contemplating grey featureless waters. Scattered on a nearby knoll are the flattened remains of a fishing hut blown down in a gale – panels of tin roofing and splintered planks and an assortment of rubbish. A dinghy lies upturned on the grass.

I cut across moorland to where the ground dips abruptly into a narrow gully and a burn gushes over a tiny fall. Hanging across the burn is a tall gate-like structure designed to stop animals from escaping along the watercourse. The barrier itself isn't old – it replaces an original – but the rusted hawser supporting it, spanning the gully, belongs to an earlier era, as do the five hefty iron hooks on which the structure hangs. Winans' work – the handiwork of a bygone age.

Winans was no sportsman. Not for him the arduous stalk on foot in pursuit of a single chosen stag. He organised deer hunts on a prodigious scale, with great numbers of the animals driven into a dead-end defile where he and his mounted companions might slaughter them at will. There was talk of a Gatling machine gun and questions were asked in parliament.

Winans scandalised the shooting fraternity by his bloodthirsty methods and angered them for his querulous resort to litigation on the slightest pretext. In the end, having been bested in court over a trifle, he quit the killing fields of Affric to live out the rest of his life in Brighton.

The Iron Fence, his legacy to the Highlands, was left to decay or to be adapted to more peaceful ends.

A week later, I struggle cross-country through dense heather and high bracken and ford a burn where it rushes noisily over shallows. A new deer fence is silhouetted against the sky.

The track from my little fishing loch is sadly changed. The fine walking route of just a week ago has been gouged by stalkers' vehicles into a rutted morass of mud and black peat. What have you done, Mr Kwint? Your 'Walkers welcome' rings hollow now.

Under an overcast sky, the brown moorland is bleak and uninviting. As the main track sweeps away to the south, a white post and a small cairn – just a heap of few stones – point the way to Loch Affric. Some way along this minor track, at a high vantage point, there stands a sturdy iron corner post, well over head height, bearing on its shank a battery of rust-bitten cogwheels – the stretchers which once held the fence wires in tension. Some twists of rusty wire still dangle from it in looped disarray. In the distance, I can see a corner of Loch Affric and, closer, there's a small lochan amid clusters of pine trees. In this lonely spot – a rusting memorial to William Winans and his failed dream of Highland empire.

Heading down to the Affric shore, I hear the sound of gunfire. Someone on the foreshore near Affric lodge is engaged in shooting practice. 'Crack, crack!' goes the rifle at regular intervals and the sound of it follows me all the way along the narrows and down to the bridge near the car park. 'Crack, crack!' – muffled now.

It's not good for your hearing, marksman. You may go deaf.

'Crack! Crack!'

87

Winans died in Brighton on 23 June 1897 but I search the newspaper archive in vain for a mention of his death. It was his posthumous misfortune to breathe his last at the time when Queen Victoria was celebrating her Diamond Jubilee. The loyal columns of the *Glasgow Herald*, for one, were filled to bursting with accounts of the event and Winans' demise failed to make the edition.

On the web I find that William had a son, Walter, who lived in Britain all his adult life and successfully assumed the role of English gentleman. He spoke with an impeccable accent, sported Dundreary whiskers and tipped a jaunty bowler hat. He had something of an artistic bent too – he sculpted horses. Like his father, he had a taste for blood sport on a grand scale. An expert shot, he declared that he hoped to kill at least one specimen of every game animal on earth.

'I have shot over a thousand stags,' he told an interviewer from the *New York Times* on his single brief visit to the States (to see a horse show). Possibly a fair proportion of his thousand stags were shot on his father's range in West Affric.

Walter met his end in 1910. While pony trotting, he crossed the finishing line slumped in his sulky and was declared dead with the reins still clasped in his lifeless hands.

Slowly the Winans fence decays. Long sections have been uprooted and, here and there, its rusty iron posts have been adapted to buttress a modern deer fence erected to keep today's deer not in but out of forest land.

There's a radio programme *A History of the World in 100 Objects*. The piece of rusting ironmongery I found in the Affric hills could surely qualify as one of a hundred objects in the history of the Highlands.

88

Descending from the Hill Lochs (still looking out for telltale signs of Iron Fence as I go), I come on a Land Rover slewed across the road. The driver's a big-made man with working hands – nails edged with black, I notice – who says his name's Younie, John Younie – strange surname. He farms at Drumnadrochit but rents grazing up here. He has sheep on the ground and later this month he'll bring cattle.

It would be fine apart from the ticks. 'Last year, I lost 90 sheep through ticks,' he says. Tick infestation seems to occur in pockets – 'Bad here but there are none in Drumnadrochit.'

Ticks can carry lime disease which attacks the nervous system – a bad business. They cling to the heather and bracken and rub off on your legs as you brush by (the spores of bracken are carcinogenic, too – nature's not always benign). I shan't wear shorts.

'Here's one,' says John, grabbing Minnie his lively collie by the scruff and prizing a bloated insect from the nape of her neck. He climbs down with the tick between his thumb and forefinger, drops it on the ground and grinds it under his heel. There's an orangey splat on the tarmac – Minnie's blood.

'You can get stuff at Tesco's to rub on your skin and it works,' he says. 'I rubbed it on my hands and I didn't get a bite after that.'

There are ways of dealing with ticks. They burrow under the skin and you have to extract them whole. It's said they'll disengage smartly if you touch them with a lighted match but I don't fancy that. Besides, I don't carry matches.

George at Upper Glassburn says John Younie used to deliver coal as a sideline to his farming. He arrived at George's place at midnight in a downpour of rain, his face streaked with coal dust black as sin. The huge truck with its flashing lights couldn't get up the awkward bend in the drive so George and he howked up several tons of coal on their backs.

George paid by cheque which John crumpled in his coaly hands and stuffed in a pocket, damp and dirty, along with his scruffy wad of notes.

'Your bank manager won't thank you for that,' says George.

'He doesn't,' says John.

89

For once, the post office at Tomich is open when I pass by. Out of curiosity, I peer in. Joyce, who works for Donald Fraser at Guisachan cottages, stands behind the counter. It's tiny – hardly more than a cubicle – and it's a time capsule. The clock stopped in the 1940s.

Old wartime posters brown with age cover the woodchip walls, urging customers to join the Wrens or the RAF or the Royal Observer Corps, or to save for victory, or send a telegram to the forces overseas at a cheap rate. On another wall, a blue line on a large map shows Donald Fraser's progress round the world in the *Spirit of Affric*, the boat he built himself, tracing his way across the Atlantic, through the Panama Canal and into the Pacific via the Antipodes and on towards the Red Sea.

It's too late, of course, to invest in the war bonds advertised on the wall. I buy stamps instead.

90

Straight off the wall, almost, news of *Spirit of Affric* and all who sail in her. Ian from Comar Lodge tells me he's just back home from India after a spell on board with Donald and his crew mate. He was at sea for two months not counting the landfalls. The longest spell at sea was nine days. He says he was never seasick – a bit queasy once or twice when the waves were 14 feet high. Before he came aboard they'd been the size of a house so he missed the worst of it. Even so, he hurt his back when thrown across the cabin. 'There's not a lot of room in a 40-foot boat,' he says.

He says Donald's voyage is part of an event called the Blue Water Rally, which is not a race but, roughly speaking, a loose convoy of boats circumnavigating the world. They keep in touch every day and meet at designated marinas. Yachties appear to be a gregarious bunch – once ashore, he says, you go out for a drink, meal, a nightcap on a neighbour's boat. In bed by midnight all the same.

91

Who's that man with the mahogany legs? A man in shorts whose wiry legs are the colour of old leather has been talking to the lady in the Cannich shop. 'They're the brownest legs I've ever seen,' I say when he's gone.

'That's Richard,' says she. 'He's a great walker. He's out on the hills every day. He's never at home.'

Richard lives in the first house past the bridge at Cannich, on a steep hillside. I've driven past many times and never noticed it half-hidden among trees.

Today he's at home – tomorrow he's off to Wales and more hills. I open the gate and climb the many steps to his door. He leads me into the kitchen, which is bachelor untidy. 'A coffee?' Where's the coffee? He searches in cupboards, finds the jar at last, drops a spoonful in a mug and rummages in a drawer. 'There are biscuits here somewhere.' He finds a crumpled packet.

'A broken biscuit is fine,' I say.

Through the kitchen window, he keeps an eye on the birds. (Birdseed is plainly easier to locate than biscuits.) 'I can flick a nut out of the window and a chaffinch will take it on the wing,' he says. Yesterday a great spotted woodpecker visited. One of the pleasures of hillwalking is the chance it gives him to watch and listen to the birds. One day in Glen Strathfarrar, he picked up the faint cry of a ring ouzel, a summer visitor to the mountains, which he reckons must have carried across two miles from a corrie on Mam Sodhail.

His living room is sparsely furnished except for one item – a handsome old grandfather clock (which *was* his grandfather's) in the corner that strikes the hour with a wheeze and a gentle tuning-fork chime. A pair of time-worn binoculars lie ready on the window sill. His boots rest against the log basket by the black stove.

Richard bought the house and land when it was going cheap shortly after he quit his job with the Forestry Commission 20 years ago. The lure of working outdoors had been dulled by too much wearisome planting of trees from a sack on his back and too many hours spent cooped up in a transit van with a squad of heavy smokers.

We take a walk around his two acres of steeply sloping ground, where he's made a semblance of order out of wilderness. He cleared narrow winding paths through the undergrowth and, over the years, has dug out most of the whin – the last of it, reprieved, glows in vibrant yellow bloom on a bank. Bracken's a curse. He stoops to tug out a frond unfurling at his feet and picks up a switch of birch to whack off any other sign of rogue growth.

He points to a seedling horse chestnut which, he says, he'll transplant to a better spot and an oak sapling threatened by small trees and brushwood around it. He'll clear the brush and give the oak space.

Among the trees high above the house is the wooden summer-house he built as a vantage point, with a mattress inside for reclining on while enjoying the view over sunlit river and strath. It's a refuge, too, when the midges are bad.

Richard has 'done' all the Munros, some of them many times. Did he say *hundreds* of times? Surely not. There are only 360-odd walking days in the year, for goodness sake!

Now he's ticking off the Marilyns. This is a technical term, like Munro, and just as pointless. A Marilyn, he explains, is a hill of any size so long as it's at least 150 metres (or 492 feet) high with a rise of at least 150 metres from base to summit all round, no matter from which side you approach it. In other words, it's a peak and not a lump. According to this crazy definition, Ben Nevis is a Marilyn but Cairn Gorm is not.

There are numerous Marilyns in Scotland, England, Wales, Ireland and the Isle of Man (the qualifying countries) and Richard calculates he has only 32 to go, including the stacs of St Kilda, the island far off the west coast – a severe challenge. He's currently working out how to get there and how to climb them. One problem is to find a safe landing place and another is the attitude of the National Trust for Scotland which discourages climbing in case it disturbs the cliff-nesting seabirds.

Has he a favourite hill in these parts? Yes – Sgorr na Diollaid in Glen Cannich. It's 818 metres high and he's climbed it many times and in all weathers. For Richard, it's a morning or afternoon jaunt. From the bailey bridge, it takes him two hours up and down. 'You just follow your nose,' he says – there's no track.

I look it up in my hill book: 'A fine little rocky peak with particularly good views of the Strathfarrar, Mullardoch and Glen Affric hills.' It sounds enticing but I'm running out of time. Right now I have another hill in mind.

There's a shadow. Richard tells me that he has inherited a gene which in the end will severely curtail his active life. This surely explains his obsessive pursuit of the heights: forever walking, climbing, scrambling. He's a driven man.

92

No Name Hill, as I call it, is a small rounded heathery hill on the high ground between Glen Affric and Glen Cannich, anonymous on the map. There's no hurry. I'm walking by 12 o' clock on a good rough stony track. I have a hazel rod picked up in the woods for a stick. It has a mossy tuft at the top and a kink that fits the hand nicely.

Big snowy hills come into view, the white bulk of Tom a' Choinich (Hill of the Moss) filling the horizon ahead and the long ridge of Toll Creagach (Rocky Hollow) stretching to its right. They're not for today. Across the river gorge the ground is spattered with snow but here it seems like summer as a butterfly – a peacock – tempted by the sun rises from the verge and then another of a different kind which I can't identify. Catherine could if she were here.

Runnels of water cross the path, leaving puddles in which stones gleam reddish and blue under the surface. There's a sputtering in the water – two long-legged frogs in a clinch, tumbling over and over in tight embrace.

A little cairn of two or three stones marks where the track to the top turns upwards. Track? Where is it? It's clearly marked with zigzags on the map – a good stalker's path, you might guess – but on the ground it's shy to the point of invisibility. I press onwards between heathery banks. The ground is soft and yielding and there's much water. Somewhere nearby, an unseen trickle of a burn clatters noisily through peaty hollows.

Larger patches of soft snow streak the hillside. Deer, startled by my sudden appearance over a small crest, turn to stare with pricked ears before fleeing – eight in a row outlined against the sky as they canter over the ridge. In another season, this would anger stalking folk but, this being March, they're safe. A little later a dozen more deer resting in a hollow turn tail and scamper away.

Mica glints in the flat stones paving the mossy summit, good to walk on. At the top, I find a stone shelter, a rectangle of drystone walls four or five feet high with an opening in one side. I speculate on its use. Was it shelter for stalkers or watchmen stationed there on the lookout for poachers?

Tom a' Choinich looms close. Two lochs are in view. Looking southwards into Glen Affric I see a long reach of Loch Beinn a'Mheadhoin with dark pinewoods reflected in the still water. A lochan sparkles on top of a bare ridge above the treeline. To the north, the last bends of the road in Glen Cannich are visible as it winds towards Loch Mullardoch – a hazy blue spread of water terminated by the grey bar of the dam. That ugliest of dams looks curiously small and fragile from this height.

I take a different line of descent, ignoring the few rickety little cairns which may or may not mark the line of the supposed zigzag path, picking my own way down. Water gurgles through a snow-filled gully, unseen for the most part except where dark holes reveal its winding course under the snow. At the bottom of one deep hole, I see where the small stream tumbles over a little stony fall. Suppose I fell through, unsuspecting? Up to the armpits, struggle to get out? I take it at a leap.

I eat my lunch seated on top of a boulder shaped like a wedge of cheese and watch a walker, coming from the Tom or the Toll perhaps, striding homewards along the track below, the only human I've seen. By the time I reach the track he's far ahead and we never meet.

93

It's cold this morning with a keen wind blowing, just on the edge of comfort. Russell leads the way with long easy strides, stick in hand and rifle over his shoulder. He's in charge of stalking for the Forestry Commission in the west of Scotland (too many deer and the forest will suffer) and today we're high in Glen Affric.

His young dog Gus, a German wirehaired pointer impatient to be running, circles round his legs. The dog's old predecessor died recently.

'This one's still got a lot to learn,' says Russell, keeping him in check. The dog's coat, typical of the breed, is a coarse dusky brown threaded with white hairs, which makes him look older than his years. He has topaz eyes.

'All our forestry stalkers have dogs as part of the job,' Russell says. 'You may not see a thing in the trees but the dog will know. A good dog will stand and point with his head when he scents deer.'

Down a rough slope we go towards a small stretch of water, Loch nan Sean-each. Two blackcock flying in close formation zip along the edge of the loch showing a flash of white underwing. Running east to west along the lochside is a line of tall rusted iron stanchions supported by angled braces. Old friends, almost – I recognise them as a remnant of the great Iron Fence that William Winans made.

We contour round a craggy heather-covered hillock called Meall Dubh (Black Lump) and raise binoculars to scan the ground ahead, a broad descending valley with scant clusters of pine trees where Russell says the hinds often congregate. The feeding is good there possibly because, in plantation days, the ground was fertilised. But today we're too late and the deer have moved on.

Deer have a regular feeding cycle, Russell says – roughly three hours feeding followed by two hours when they rest and chew the cud. He says that if you know their habits and their feeding pattern, you'll find them. And he's confident that he will –'Ninety-five per cent sure of a kill,' he says.

We tramp through high heather round Meall Dubh and suddenly, as we round the crag, we're in a milder climate, sheltered from the piercing wind and warmed by the emerging sun. A reach of Loch Beinn a'Mheadhoin lies below.

Russell slips a cord round Gus's neck to keep him close and we enter the pinewood that cloaks the steep slope (this is where the deer shelter after feeding) and make our way slowly through the trees, picking our steps, not talking. Where Russell goes I follow, slithering down a muddy slope, brushing through bracken, ducking under a branch, stretching across a small burn, hoisting myself up a grassy bluff. Russell stops, crouches, beckons and points below. 'Sika deer,' he whispers. Just one and it's gone in an instant, slipping into the trees far below before I can catch sight of it. I lack the practised eye.

I remark on the black metal sleeve round the rifle barrel, which he says it to muffle the sound of the shot. 'If you're firing every day it affects your hearing. Mine's not as good as it was. All stalkers are deaf.'

We sit on a patch of open ground and Russell sweeps the whole slope. He spots a small group of red deer running close to the shoreline but only fleetingly. Again I don't. We resume climbing and find another lookout spot among the rocky outcrops on the eastern face of Meall Dubh, where we perch for another survey. In front of us, a bare notched ridge leads the eye to the rocky top of Beinn nan Sparra. Three lochans glint along the spine of the ridge, the last and largest of which is Loch an Eang. As for deer, we draw a blank. None to be seen.

The circuit of Meall Dubh has brought us back in sight of our vehicle and Russell proposes driving over to the top end of Loch Beinn a'Mheadhoin to see what we can find there.

Once there we walk through a fine stand of open pine trees. Here, says Russell, the Forestry Commission hoped to promote natural regeneration from the fall of seed. They lost heart when too few seedlings appeared and resorted to planting among the existing trees. These planted trees are tall now and to the untrained eye they look natural enough. With the afternoon sun shining through the tracery, it's a true walk in the woods – and a far cry from stalking on the open hill.

Somewhere for sure there are deer. Gus, good dog, has the scent. He holds his head high and his nostrils twitch but no deer show. The pine gives way to birch, many of the trees old and twisted, many damaged, snapped at the stem or fallen to the ground where they lie in various stages of decomposition. Broken branches and twigs littler the ground.

This is not easy walking. Russell treads softly, delicately, slowly, and I follow a couple of yards behind, trying to avoid snapping twigs as I go. Once again, we've fallen silent. The loudest sound is the panting of the dog.

At the end of the day, there's nothing to show. Not a shot was fired. But from my point of view it's been a good day out. We got fresh chill winds and sun's warmth on our faces in equal measure. And no creature died because of us.

94

I knock on the door at the sad hotel and Louise asks me in. Inside the lobby, there's a bale of straw or hay smelling of the farmyard. I crunch over broken floor tiles. The furniture's in disarray, easy chairs crammed into a corner of a barren room – the dining room I think it was in better days. In the kitchen, a young man tinkers with an odd-looking apparatus consisting of a green oil drum set on a table from which plastic tubes connect with glass bottles on the floor.

'He's making bio-fuel,' Louise remarks as we pass through to the wing of the old hotel which has been acquired by someone from the south and now functions as a pub. Leaning on her elbows at the bar, sweeping back her hair with one hand and gesturing with the other, she fixes me in the eye and talks earnestly about her love–hate affair with the hotel, the village, the folk, and her mission in life. She could write a book about it, she says – the title to be *You Think I'm Mad but I can Help*.

Well, many people think her off-the-wall. As for me, I enjoy listening to her dreams. She's a visionary. I like Louise and I'm not alone. George at Upper Glassburn has a soft spot for her. 'You can't fail to like and admire her in a funny kind of way,' he said. 'She's endlessly cheerful – she brightens up the day.'

The hotel is open house. It seems that people drop in, stay for a while, opt in, opt out, leave. Currently resident are a South African girl and her boyfriend the bio-fuel man.

Louise says she aims to help people in need –'rescuing' is her word for it. Among those she has rescued are the 30 Poles who worked in a fish factory in Dingwall and ended up with nowhere to stay. Louise put them up. The council didn't like it, muttering darkly of multi-occupancy and unimpressed by her claim to be running a legitimate hotel. Court action was threatened and the electricity cut off. The Poles left by candlelight.

'Did you know I'd been living on a croft in Sutherland?' she asks brightly. No, I didn't. She went there for a spell. It was one of those times when her feelings about Cannich tipped to the dark side and she took flight with her horse and a Shetland pony – I imagine her tramping north à la Stevenson with his donkey but I guess she got transport.

Back in Affric, her plans develop. Currently, she intends to invite volunteers to help her renovate the hotel, in return for which they'll be offered a timeshare in the place.

'Perhaps you'd like to volunteer?' she asks brightly.

Darkly, I gaze into my glass.

95

There's shouting. I walk across to the Cannich shinty park and find a game in progress.

It's a rough business – a sort of mad hockey.

A lofted ball loops high very nearly the whole length of the long pitch. Sticks clash overhead or whack on shins. One player takes the ball full on the chest, stops it dead. Heart-stopping, more like. There are bruising encounters but no one seems to feel the pain.

Two swallows flit across the field. On the horizon, a large black bird circles in wide sweeps above the treetops. I think it may be an eagle. But as they say, if you only think, then it's not.

It's all action on the pitch but on the sidelines we supporters – in groups of twos and threes and two dogs – lean on a gate or loll on the grass or, in the case of the dogs, express lordly indifference. Hills, trees, river, puffy white clouds in a sky of blue – the scene is idyllic. It's possible, if you try, not to notice the pylon at the corner of the field.

Half-time and a grey-headed veteran comes along rattling a plastic bucket with coins in the bottom. 'For team funds,' he says.

Did he play? 'Forty-five years ago, fifty. You had a struggle to get in the team in those days, not like now. If you were seen out and about on a Friday night, you were out of the team for Saturday.'

It's the second team today.

'What are the first team like?'

'Bottom of the league,' says he, 'and last year they were top.' Like the shinty ball, their fortunes rise and fall with rocket-like velocity.

Life's like that, sometimes.

POSTSCRIPT

It's five years since I last spent time in Strathfarrar and the glens and, since then, there have been changes. The people I met grow older and some are gone.

Donald the Blue Charm died in hospital at the age of 93, felled by a stroke. His brother Duncan – 'Dunky Affric' to all, Old Duncan as I have called him – is frail but as I write lives on at 99, having seen his memoir *My Yester Years in Glen Affaric* published locally to acclaim. It's now in its second edition – a delightful account of a stalker's life in past times, in harmony with the outdoors. Duncan's son John – 'Johnny Affric' – though semi-retired, still goes out on the hill. Another John, founder of the Cougie dynasty, who was unwell when I last met him, has died.

Sister Petra Clare, 'hermit iconographer' as she styles herself, has had to scale down her vision of a colony of hermitages centred on the church at Marydale. I suspect that the Church authorities were cool. Much of her effort now is devoted to setting up a charity to promote links between the western Catholic and eastern Orthodox churches and she is also concerned with encouraging what she calls the liturgical arts – everything pertaining to the ornamentation of churches from vestments and altar cloths to silverware. And she continues to make her glorious icons.

Louise lives on bravely in her distressed home which used to be the hotel at Cannich, solitary but still exuding universal goodwill. She has a part-time job at a new equestrian centre which has been established south of Cannich where it's a joy to see her skill with and affection for horses, including her own Fritz. She's the nearest to a horse whisperer I know.

Among other changes, the Forestry Commission has called time on the wild boar experiment and the piggies have gone. Deanie, the last Lovat outpost in Glen Strathfarrar, has been sold to the neighbouring

Braulen Estate and Scott, who lived there, has moved on, leaving his grove of alphabetical Celtic trees to flourish for others. I hope he took his compost.

As required by protocol, the coat of arms 'by royal appointment' at Campbell's tweed shop in Beauly has been taken down after serving its time – a small loss to the High Street. And Tim's daffodil-coloured vintage Porsche is for sale – 'Time to put away the toys,' as he says.

On the larger scale, a public enquiry ruled that the Beauly–Stirling power line should go ahead as planned and now mammoth pylons stalk across the countryside, even in some places thrusting above the skyline. Some former opponents now admit that you get used to them, to the extent of not even realising their existence, others damn them for their intrusion – a sentiment I share.

But the hills and the skies are changeless and the magic remains.